ENVIRONMENTAL
AWARENESS
CASE STUDIES

*Contributing
Environmental Writers*

Burkhard Bilger
Robert F. Ehrhardt
Gloria J. Dyer
Robert T. Calandra Jr.

*Printed on
recycled paper.*

 D.C. Heath and Company
Lexington, Massachusetts/Toronto, Ontario

Executive Editor: Ceanne P. Tzimopoulos
Supervising Editor: Christine H. Wang
Project Editor: Andrew L. Amster,
Editorial Development: Amy R. Pallant, Ann E. Bekebrede
Design Management and Cover Design: Lisa Fowler
Composition in Quark: Ricki Pappo
Illustrations: Camille Venti
Production Coordinator: Maureen Bisso
Cover Photographs: © Terry Donnelly, Tom Stack & Associates
Earth, © Telegraph Colour Library 199, FPG International

ENVIRONMENTAL WRITERS

Burkhard Bilger is author of *Global Warming* (Chelsea House Publishers, 1991) and Senior Editor of *Earthwatch*, a bimonthly magazine of field science and the environment. A graduate of Yale University, Bilger has earned two gold medals from the Regional Magazine Publishers Association and honorable mention for the 1992 Evert Clark Award for Science Journalism. He has joined and reported on research projects in Tunisia, Mallorca, Poland, Russia, Namibia, and a number of other countries.

Robert F. Ehrhardt, C.E.P., is past president and former Chairman of the Board of National Association of Environmental Professionals. His work experience includes assignments at the Environmental Studies Board of the National Academy of Sciences, the environmental consulting firm of Dames & Moore, and the Corporate Environmental Programs department of General Electric Corporation.

Gloria J. Dyer, Ed.D. teaches environmental studies courses at Fairleigh Dickinson University in New Jersey.

Robert T. Calandra Jr. is a freelance writer specializing in medical and science writing.

Copyright © 1994 by D.C. Heath and Company

Permission to reproduce these pages for classroom use is granted to users of D.C. Heath science textbooks.

Published simultaneously in Canada
Printed in the United States of America

International Standard Book Number: 0-669-30820-X

Table of Contents

What is Environmental Awareness?   2
Becoming Environmentally Aware   4

Case Study 1   **Ozone: Crisis Averted?**   8
     Looks at the ozone "hole" as a subject of scientific debate. Scientists appear to disagree on what might be a threat to the global environment.

Case Study 2   **The James Bay Project**   16
     A look at how a massive hydroelectric project in Canada pits the need for clean, cheap energy against the interests of the Native inhabitants of Québec.

Case Study 3   **A Burning Question**   26
     Examines the issue of hazardous waste disposal as viewed through the eyes of the residents of East Liverpool, Ohio — site of a hazardous waste incinerator.

Case Study 4   **Acid on the Wind**   34
     Asks the question, "How are the energy needs of Midwestern and Appalachian states part of the acid rain problem experienced by New York's Adirondack Mountains?"

Case Study 5   **Something in the Water**   42
     Looks at the careful balancing act between business and agriculture and the effects of land use on groundwater resources.

Case Study 6   **No Room in the Bin**   50
     How do decisions made by McDonald's reflect the growing concern and awareness of the problems of solid waste disposal?

Case Study 7   **Rain Forests Under Siege**   60
     In the rain forests of Ecuador, how are the rights of indigenous peoples and the need to preserve biodiversity balanced against Ecuador's economic needs?

Case Study 8   **Trouble in the Sound**   68
     Examines the pollution of New York's Long Island Sound — the sources of the trouble and the tough decisions involved in remedying them.

Almanac   76
Appendix
     Expressing an Educated Opinion   88
     Resources for Further Study   90
     Graphing Skills   91

WHAT IS *Environmental* AWARENESS?

by Burkhard Bilger

The planet's weather patterns are so sensitive, it's been said, that air currents caused by a butterfly flapping its wings in Bangkok could end up causing a tornado over Topeka. It's a sobering thought — if a bit farfetched. It is also oddly reassuring. Each of us matters. We are all part of a world community and, as such, the actions of individuals can have worldwide consequences. For example, many of the environmental problems we see today are the result of careless and wasteful individual actions. At the same time, solutions to some of those problems can begin with the action of one person.

For a good deal of our history, humans have placed themselves apart from nature rather than within it. During the Renaissance, western philosophers and theologians saw humans as part of a "Great Chain of Being." The chain began, at its lowest level, with mosses and plants. The chain worked its way up through clams, fish, reptiles, birds, mammals, and finally reached humans. Humans, because of their place at the highest level of the chain, considered themselves superior to all other species. The decisions and actions of people in the Renaissance reflected this view of the world. The view has not changed much in the centuries since the Renaissance. People in industrialized society make decisions based on the mistaken notions that there are no limits to Earth's resources, that humans are superior to other living things, and that Earth can absorb human wastes. However, a growing number of people are showing that humans are in fact a part of nature. Despite all our technology, we still depend on Earth's ecosystems for food, health, and shelter. We could not live without Earth's resources — its air, water, and soil.

Realizing our place in nature and taking responsibility for it can be a challenge. Does my refrigerator contain CFCs that destroy ozone? Is the electricity for my reading light generated by a coal-burning power plant? Was the coal removed from a strip-mine that destroyed the nesting grounds of endangered birds? Most of us don't have time to answer every question about our actions and their effect on the environment. Yet everyone wants to breathe clean air and drink uncontaminated water. So we look to environmental groups for advice. *Recycle! Conserve energy! Buy organic produce! Don't buy tropical hardwoods! Become a vegetarian!* These groups ask us to change our lifestyles and the way we view and treat Earth. Much of their advice is good, but not all of it. For example, some citizen-action

groups have been known to adopt environmental-sounding names even if they favor destructive development. Some corporations now make their products seem friendly to the environment, whether they are or not. Even environmental groups may have principles more radical than your own. What changes in your lifestyle are you willing to make in order to reduce your environmental impact? Whose advice do you listen to? Environmental decisions are too important to make on faith and too difficult for simple slogans to resolve.

Environmental awareness requires more than just being concerned. Environmental awareness requires information and understanding. You need to know the facts to understand the issue. To justify reducing or controlling acid rain with stricter air pollution regulations, you have to know how doing so would affect coal miners in West Virginia. Before you protest the building of a hydroelectric dam, you should know how much pollution the oil-, coal-, or nuclear-powered plants needed to replace the dam would produce. As you become more informed about environmental issues, you may find that you ask even more environmental questions. How can debt-ridden, tropical countries absorb the costs of protecting their rain forests? Which endangered species should we save with limited funds for environmental protection?

It's impossible to know how everything you do affects the environment. But you can learn where society does the most environmental damage and how you can diminish your part in it. Your first responsibility is to your own ecosystem. Saving the giant panda may sound like an exciting cause, but you can probably do more good saving newspapers for your neighborhood's recycling program. The most important part of being environmentally aware is understanding that each person matters. Who knows? Like the butterfly flapping its wings in Bangkok, your small action may start a movement that sweeps halfway across the world.

BECOMING *Environmentally* AWARE

The case studies in this book deal with issues that hinge upon the wise use and protection of Earth's environment. You are well aware of how important decisions about environmental issues can be. You also may be aware of just how *complicated* those decisions can be. Taking an educated position on environmental issues requires getting the facts, evaluating what you are being told, and thinking critically about all points of view.

USING A CASE STUDY

A case study is an article used to illustrate a large or complex issue. A case can focus on one location — for example, a single town — and the specific problems of that one location and the people who live there. A case study allows you to focus on those problems in detail. The facts in the case and the decision-making skills used to evaluate the problems and solutions can then be used to look at similar problems elsewhere.

These *Environmental Awareness* case studies are designed to help you dig deeper into areas of environmental concern. The features in each case study should help you analyze the problems and decide on possible solutions. Those features are described below.

Introduction Read the *Introduction* first when you come to a new case study. The *Introduction* will give you a preview of the issue being discussed in the case, the location and people involved, and whether the problem is a subject of debate.

Getting Started Next read the *Getting Started* questions. Keep these questions in your mind as you read the rest of the case. The questions will help direct your attention to important topics developed in the case study.

Focus As you are reading the case study, you will sometimes encounter a small black triangle at the end of a sentence. When you come to this triangle, stop reading. Look in the margin next to the triangle, and read the *Focus* question or questions in the box. The *Focus* questions are examples of the types of questions you should ask yourself while you are reading. For instance, a *Focus* question may recommend that you question a person's motives or look more closely at the data being cited.

Connections You will find additional information that can help you understand the case issues in the *Connections* boxes in the margin. Some of the *Connections* boxes refer you to the *Almanac* in the back of the book. As you will see from the *Connections* titles, issues dealing with Earth's environment involve information from many different areas of human knowledge, including the science areas of earth science, biology, chemistry, and physics. The scientific information provided in this book is only a starting point. Follow your interests and look into these other subjects in greater depth. The more you know about the science behind the headlines, the better you will be able to make sound decisions about environmental issues.

Analysis Once you have finished reading the case study, the *Analysis* section will help you evaluate what you have read and form opinions about the larger issue the case represents. The *Analysis* section will invite you to ask the following questions:

- What is the problem in this case?
- What are the possible solutions to that problem?
- Are there different sides in this case?
- What companies, groups, or individuals are on which side of the issue and why?
- What scientific data have been used to justify positions in the case? Does that data seem valid? Are there data missing that you need to arrive at an informed opinion?
- Is evidence from the various sides of the issue contradictory?

Working through the case study and the *Analysis* section may allow you to take a position on the larger environmental problem and the possible solutions. Perhaps you will want to gather more information. In the end, you will be more informed and will have thought about the complexities behind today's environmental headlines.

COST–BENEFIT ANALYSIS

Once you have identified the problem, gathered sufficient information, and examined possible solutions, your next step is to decide on your position. Should some action be taken? Which action would you recommend? When and how rapidly should this action be taken? What can you do personally to see to it that your idea contributes to a solution of the problem?

One approach to analyzing a complicated problem is to list the pros and cons. A related method of evaluating problems and solutions is called a *cost–benefit analysis*. To use this method to decide about difficult environmental issues, try asking yourself the following questions:

What are the costs?
What are the benefits?

These two questions should be asked about both the problem and the proposed solutions. Sometimes costs are obvious, such as the amount of money it would take to equip an old factory with modern air pollution controls. But remember that "costs" are not always measured in terms of money. For example, a job that is time-consuming costs you the time you could have spent doing something else. A town whose citizens' health is declining is paying a cost. The extinction of a species is a cost. The inability to use a lake for fishing or for swimming is also a cost.

Benefits are the flip-side of this same coin. Doing something that would improve your health, raise your income, create jobs, encourage ecosystems to thrive, clean air or water that was once polluted — all of these would be benefits. In a simple situation, an action is worth taking if the benefits are greater than the costs. However, most environmental problems do not have simple solutions.

How much time does it take to receive the benefits or to pay the costs?

Time is the first complication to many otherwise simple cost–benefit analyses. Are the costs short-term costs or long-term costs? Do the benefits start immediately or are they realized over a long period? The amount of time can affect the affordability of an action. Paying a few extra dollars for pollution clean-up on a water bill over ten years is easier than paying hundreds of dollars all at once today.

Time can also affect how you perceive the action and its consequences. For instance, a large cost paid over a long period may not only be more affordable but also may *seem* like less of a burden. On the other hand, people or companies may not want to pay large costs for a solution today if they won't see the benefits for many decades.

Who pays the costs?
Who receives the benefits?

These two questions touch on issues of social and economic fairness. Sometimes the people who receive most of the benefits from an environmental action are not the same people who bear most of the costs. An industry might pay millions of dollars to clean up a lake for the benefit of the local ecosystems or the recreational users. A farmer might get the benefits of increased crop yield by using pesticides, but nearby residents might pay the costs of having pesticides from the farmer's fields contaminate their well water.

Many environmental problems do not remain local. Pollutants in the air and water move from town to town or across state and national boundaries. For instance, eastern Canada and the northeast United States have paid the environmental costs for acid rain caused, in part, by coal-burning power plants in Midwestern states. Some problems become everybody's responsibility. Hazardous and solid wastes are transported from state to state and country to country. Tax dollars paid to the federal government by people all across the country get used to clean up toxic waste sites in relatively few places.

When thinking about environmental issues, you may ask yourself if the divisions of costs and benefits are fair. If they don't seem fair, do other considerations outweigh the questions of fairness?

Are the benefits worth the costs?

Sometimes the cost of something is simply too much. You wouldn't pay $50 to see a movie or buy an ice-cream cone. Similarly, some environmental solutions may cost too much to be practical. A solution to air pollution that would bankrupt and shut down the automobile industry would plunge hundreds of thousands of people in the United States out of work. While the benefit of having no more smog or air pollution from car exhaust is desirable, the economic impact of such an action is not acceptable.

Let's look at another example. Imagine that there is a sewage treatment plant releasing pollutants into a river. The town needs to decide how much money to spend on installing pollution controls at the treatment plant. Spending a certain amount of money will clean up the wastewater 50 percent. Spending 4 times that amount will clean up the water 75 percent. To get an 85 percent clean-up takes an expenditure of 20 times the initial amount. It will take 100 times the initial amount of money to get a 90 percent clean-up. No one knows how much money it will take to purify the water complely before releasing it into the river. In this example, the initial amount of money is in the millions of dollars. The hard choice for the town is deciding how much benefit is worth how much cost. Is there enough of a difference between an 85 percent and a 90 percent clean-up to justify spending the additional money?

Sometimes using cost–benefit analysis to look at an environmental issue will strike you as an oversimplified way of looking at an emotionally charged, complex situation. For instance, not everything has a cost you can quantify. What value do you put on beautiful scenery or on the survival of a single species? That value is also highly personal. Estimating future costs and benefits is also difficult. Finally, a typical analysis has so many variables that a person's or a company's bias can slant the results.

While there are drawbacks to using cost–benefit analysis, you may find that it is often a good way to start. Most importantly, think critically about an environmental issue before deciding on your position. That is the essence of environmental awareness.

Ozone: Crisis Averted?

by Robert T. Calandra Jr.

GETTING STARTED

- What is the ozone layer and why is it important to life on Earth?
- What are the causes of ozone depletion? Have these causes been addressed?
- To what extent does the information reported in an article affect a reader's opinion of an environmental concern?

The problem with ozone these days is there never seems to be the right amount. The debate over ozone thinning and its effects is complex. Often the information and claims are couched in dramatic language. For example, a report from the United Nations Environmental Program states that "thinning of the global ozone layer can harm millions of people as well as the world's ecosystem." On the other hand, John E. Frederick, an atmospheric physicist at the University of Chicago, states, "People get all excited about a few-percent change in UV, but it's nothing to get a 20 percent increase naturally. If an increase of 20 percent were going to be so damaging, there should be no life in Florida."

Discovery of ozone depletion above Antarctica in the 1980s raised concerns about how this might affect life on Earth. Even though scientists disagree about the cause of ozone depletion, progress is being made to reduce the use of the chemicals that are the most responsible for ozone destruction. However, if all ozone-depleting substances were banned tomorrow, would ozone thinning no longer be a concern?

In this case study, you will examine a newspaper article about ozone depletion. The process of ozone depletion — the reduction in the number of ozone molecules in the stratosphere — is complicated. A good way to keep informed is to read newspaper and magazine articles about important environmental issues. However, this should be done with a critical eye. How are the facts being reported? Is all or just part of the research being reported? How you analyze the facts will help you decide whether or not to encourage public policy makers to deal with environmental issues.

CONNECTIONS
METEOROLOGY

For more information on the structure of the atmosphere, see the *Almanac* entry on page 78.

CASE STUDY

THE SKY HAS HOLES?

Approximately 20 to 50 kilometers above Earth's surface, a thin layer of ozone gas, O_3, surrounds Earth. This layer screens out more than 99 percent of the sun's harmful ultraviolet (UV) radiation. However, NASA satellite images have confirmed that the "hole" — that is, a thinning — in the ozone layer has appeared in the stratosphere over Antarctica.

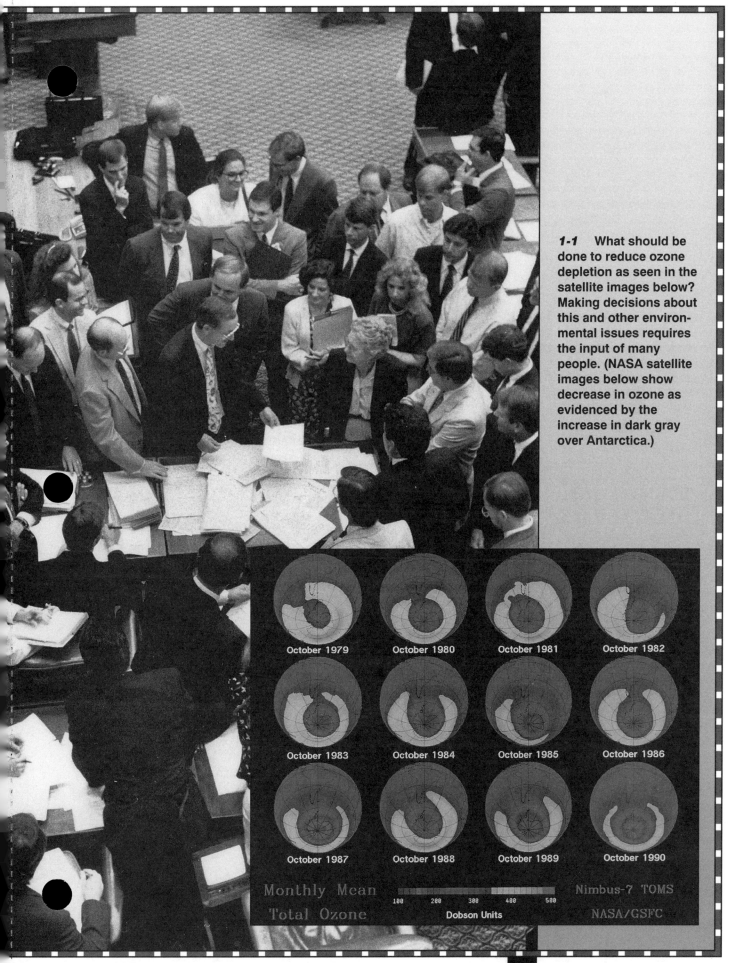

1-1 What should be done to reduce ozone depletion as seen in the satellite images below? Making decisions about this and other environmental issues requires the input of many people. (NASA satellite images below show decrease in ozone as evidenced by the increase in dark gray over Antarctica.)

From the late 1970s to the early 1990s, the ozone hole over Antarctica grew larger. This hole was sometimes as large as the United States. During the fall of 1990, the concentration of ozone over Antarctica decreased by as much as 50 percent. Researchers are now seeing signs of ozone depletion over the Northern Hemisphere as well.

TIME IN THE SUN

Humans, unprotected by scales and feathers, are vulnerable to UV radiation from the sun. In reasonable amounts, UV radiation tans skin and stimulates vitamin D production in the skin. However, it is known that excessive UV radiation increases a human's risk of getting skin cancer, cataracts, and possible immune system deficiencies. Fortunately, there are many ways for you to protect yourself from UV radiation. You can cover exposed skin, wear sunglasses, or avoid the sun.

Most animals and plants do not have any options for avoiding UV radiation. Studies done on plants show that intense UV radiation is usually lethal. Smaller amounts have been shown to inhibit photosynthesis, stunt growth, and cause mutations.

OZONE: NOW YOU SEE IT...

Ozone depletion results, in part, from the release of gases called chlorofluorocarbons (CFCs) into the atmosphere. CFCs are organic compounds containing hydrogen, carbon, chlorine, and fluorine. CFCs are used as coolants in air conditioners and refrigerators and to clean circuit boards or computers. Some CFCs were used to "puff-up" plastic foam products, like the foam in a seat cushion or the hard foam used in egg cartons. CFCs do not break apart easily. Once CFCs are released into the atmosphere, they rise from Earth's surface to the stratosphere.

In 1976, the National Aeronautics and Space Administration (NASA), the National Oceanic and Atmospheric Administration (NOAA), and the National Academy of Sciences confirmed that chlorine released from CFC molecules by UV radiation can destroy ozone. That damage may also last for decades. A single chlorine atom can destroy thousands of ozone molecules. Where ozone is depleted, larger amounts of UV radiation can reach Earth's surface.

READING INTO THE NEWS

Because of the concern over ozone depletion and the potential effects of increased UV radiation, representatives of 24 nations met in Montreal, Canada, in 1987. They developed a plan to

> **CONNECTIONS**
> **PHYSICS**
> For more information on UV radiation and the electromagnetic spectrum, see the *Almanac* entry on page 77.

> **CONNECTIONS**
> **CHEMISTRY**
> For more information on ozone, see the *Almanac* entry on page 77.

1-2 CFCs migrate to the upper stratosphere where they destroy ozone.

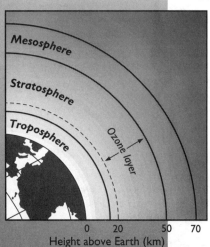

reduce the production of the eight most widely-used and most damaging CFCs. The resulting treaty is known as the Montreal Protocol. By early 1990, 49 countries had signed the treaty. If the treaty provisions are carried out, they will reduce global emissions of CFCs by 35 percent between 1989 and 2000.

The following newspaper article reports on the effects of the Montreal Protocol on the ozone problem. As you read this article, evaluate what is being said about ozone depletion. Is there an ozone problem?

1-3 These things either are or were manufactured using CFCs.

EXCERPTS FROM: **After 2000, Outlook for the Ozone Layer Looks Good.**
The Washington Post, April 15, 1993,
BY: Boyce Rensberger, Washington Post Staff Writer

After nearly a decade of headlines and hand-wringing about erosion of the Earth's protective ozone layer, the problem appears to be well on the way to solution. As a result of the Montreal Protocol, an international treaty obliging signatory countries to phase out ozone-destroying chemicals, scientists expect the threat of ozone destruction to peak in just seven years. In 2000, according to the latest scientific estimates, the ozone layer should start slowly getting thicker and better able to block the sun's harmful ultraviolet (UV) rays.

In fact, researchers say, the problem appears to be heading toward solution before they can find any solid evidence that serious harm was or is being done.

This hopeful trend — at variance with the dark scenarios of environmental doom that were pronounced after discovery of the Antarctic ozone hole in the 1980s — is supported not only by growing scientific evidence but even by scientists in the environmental movement. ▶

"The current and projected levels of ozone depletion do not appear to represent a catastrophe," said Michael Oppenheimer, an atmospheric scientist with the Environmental Defense Fund. "But I'm flabbergasted that we let it go this far before taking action. It was a potentially very serious problem."

Richard Stolarski, an atmospheric scientist at NASA's Goddard Space Flight Center, agreed: "I happen not to be of the disaster school. It's a serious concern but we can't show that anything really catastrophic has happened yet, or that anything catastrophic will happen in the future."

Attempts to detect the most feared effect of ozone depletion — increased bombardment of the Earth's surface by UV rays — have failed to turn up any evidence of increased ultraviolet influx outside the Antarctic region during the few weeks each year that the ozone hole is open. ▶

*© 1993, THE WASHINGTON POST, REPRINTED WITH PERMISSION

How could the wording of this paragraph bias the reader?

Does this mean it is OK to ignore the effects of ozone depletion around Antarctica?

If there has been any increase in UV, researchers say, it is too small to measure against a background of normal ultraviolet levels that rise and fall by large amounts for entirely natural reasons on time scales from hours to decades.

Given the expected improvements in the ozone layer, even the ozone hole eventually could stop opening. Already scientists see signs that the hole is not likely to grow much bigger than it has.

Even when the problem reaches its worst in 2000, scientists expect summertime ozone losses over temperate zones to be about 6 percent, double what they are now. Because each percentage point of ozone loss theoretically leads to an increase in UV intensity of 1.3 percentage points, the potential increase in ultraviolet would be about 8 percent.

Scientists calculate that the increased UV exposure a Washingtonian would get in midsummer then will be the equivalent of moving south about 200 miles now. In other words, if you want to know what [Washington's] ultraviolet level will be like in July 2000, go to, say, Raleigh, NC, this July.

Worst Depletion Occurs in Late Winter

"One reason we haven't seen any increase in UV is that we didn't start taking good data long ago," said Stolarski, who nearly 20 years ago was among the first researchers to assert that the ozone layer could be damaged if certain chemicals — especially chlorine — traveled high enough in the atmosphere.

Ultraviolet Rays Fluctuate Naturally

Because of natural fluctuations in ultraviolet, it is impossible to detect a trend in a short period of data collection. While there is evidence that the ozone damage is happening, it has proven impossible so far to detect any resulting increase in UV reaching the ground because ultraviolet fluctuates so much naturally. ◄

"The amount of increase that the theory says we could be getting from ozone depletion is smaller than the error of our best measuring instruments," said John E. Frederick, an atmospheric physicist at the University of Chicago.

"People get all excited about a few-percent change in UV, but it's nothing to get a 20 percent increase naturally," Frederick said. "If an increase of 20 percent were going to be so damaging, there should be no life in Florida," where ultraviolet always exceeded the allegedly dangerous levels once forecast for more northerly latitudes. ◄

FOCUS ► What are some of the causes of natural fluctuations in the ozone layer?

FOCUS ► Is an atmospheric physicist the person to listen to about the danger of UV radiation to living things?

SCIENCE BEHIND THE HEADLINES

After reading the newspaper article, were you able to come to any conclusions about ozone depletion? Do you think there is an ozone problem? Before answering these questions, think about the facts you read in the article. Then, as you continue to read this case, evaluate how additional facts on ozone depletion affect your understanding of the debate.

Liz Cook, from Friends of the Earth, an environmental group, agrees that it looks like the ozone has been saved. Yet she feels "It's a definite mistake to give an impression that the problem is whipped. It's not a problem we can wash our hands of. We're assuming everyone does what they're supposed to do." Ozone will only continue to recover if CFCs and other ozone-destroying chemicals are no longer used. This is something the article does not consider.

Until the Montreal Protocol's CFC ban takes effect in 2000, nations can keep manufacturing CFCs. Even now, plenty of people still own refrigerators, room air conditioners, and cars with air conditioners — all cooled with CFCs. As long as these products are in use or are being sent to junkyards or landfills, CFCs will continue to rise into the atmosphere.

> **CONNECTIONS**
> **BIOLOGY**
> For more information on CFCs, see the *Almanac* entry on page 77.

UNDER THE OZONE HOLE

Scientists and environmentalists agree that, to date, there is little solid evidence that Earth's ecosystems are suffering from increased UV radiation due to ozone depletion. Richard Stolarski is quoted in the article as saying "...we can't show that anything really catastrophic has happened yet, or that anything catastrophic will happen in the future." Those who study planktonic organisms in the oceans surrounding Antarctica have found evidence of a 6 to 12 percent decline in the number of phytoplankton. This decline occurs during the months when the ozone hole is open. (The ozone hole is open for only three of the twelve months.) However, when phytoplankton populations are averaged over a full year, the loss in productivity is estimated to be only 2 to 4 percent. The decline in phytoplankton has proved to be less worrisome than originally estimated.

However, people still worry about how ozone depletion may directly affect their own health. It is still theoretically possible that *any* increased ultraviolet levels due to ozone depletion may lead to an increased number of skin cancer cases. One rule of thumb scientists use is that for every decline of 1 percent in ozone, there is a 1.3 percent increase in the amount of UV radiation. As reported in the newspaper article, "Even when the problem reaches its worst in 2000, scientists expect summertime ozone losses over temperate zones to be about 6 percent... the potential increase in ultraviolet would be about 8 percent." The Environmental Protection Agency (EPA) estimates a 5 percent ozone depletion would cause the following effects in the United States: An additional 940 000 cases annually of non-fatal skin cancers and 30 000 fatal skin cancers, a sharp increase in cataracts, decreased yields of important

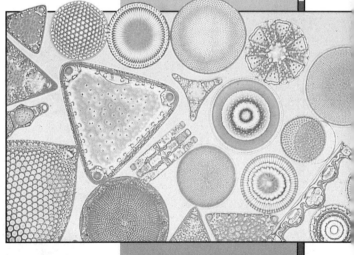

1-4 Since the ozone hole in the Antarctic was discovered, scientists have been researching how the increased UV radiation might affect phytoplankton productivity.

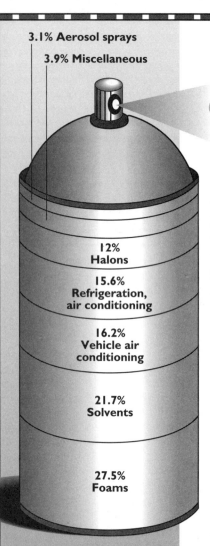

1-5 Use of ozone-depleting chemicals. (EPA 1991)

1-6 Clothing can protect you from too much ultroviolet radiation.

food crops, and a reduction in growth of phytoplankton that form the base of the ocean food chains.

Even though researchers don't know all the possible effects of UV radiation on life, it is agreed that the effects of UV radiation are cumulative. Scientists have not yet documented changes in Earth's ecosystems due to ozone depletion. But it is possible that these changes are already underway. As a precaution, many nations have responded to the threat by agreeing to phase out CFCs. The ozone layer may recover without causing major environmental damage because the international community acted before all the evidence was in.

STATING THE ISSUE

Progress is being made toward solving Earth's ozone crisis. Yet, for the immediate future, the debate continues over the extent to which ozone is being depleted. In February 1992, NASA scientists reported that the ozone layer was showing a record loss worldwide. Ozone levels over populated areas of North America, Europe, and Asia were substantially lower than had been predicted, and scientists were not quite sure why. "A lot of what we're seeing over the Northern Hemisphere is not well understood," admits Samuel Oltman, a NOAA physicist.

Differences exist in individual understanding about the ozone threat. In many instances, different conclusions can be expressed based on the evaluation of limited facts. Did your conclusions about ozone depletion change with the addition of more scientific data?

Stories about Earth's environment fill newspapers, magazines, and television and radio programs. However, both audiences and reporters have different ideas about environmental problems. As you learned in this case study on ozone depletion, factual information on environmental issues can be presented — or read — in ways that make it seem either good news or bad. Examining and thinking about what you read or see may lead to new answers. It can possibly lead to more questions.

ANALYSIS

IDENTIFY THE PROBLEM
■ What information needs to be gathered to evaluate the following excerpt from the article?

"Because of natural fluctuations in ultraviolet, it is impossible to detect a trend in a short period of data collection. While there is evidence that the ozone damage is happening, it has proven impossible so far to detect any resulting increase in UV reaching the ground because ultraviolet fluctuates so much naturally."

■ One reader of Boyce Rensberger's article *After 2000, Outlook for the Ozone Layer Looks Good* wrote, "The message I take from this article is that things will probably be OK because we saw the problem and acted." Write an essay agreeing or disagreeing with this statement.

PLOTTING THE FUTURE
■ Using the data on page 78 of the *Almanac,* graph production of CFC-12. What does this graph tell you about trends in CFC use?

LOOKING MORE CLOSELY: SCIENCE
■ Most industrialized nations — heavy users of CFCs — are located in the Northern Hemisphere. Yet the worst ozone thinning occurs in the Southern Hemisphere over Antarctica. Research the unique conditions that contribute to higher levels of ozone depletion over Antarctica.

LOOKING MORE CLOSELY: ISSUES
■ Differences exist in perceptions about the existence of environmental threats, their origins, their relative importance, and what to do about them. Find a newspaper or magazine article that presents different sides of the same controversy. Compare the two arguments and how they are used to defend different positions.

ACTING ON THE ISSUES

OZONE LOSS: PROTECTING YOURSELF

■ Do you use products that add CFCs to the atmosphere? Which, if any, of these things would you be willing to give up in order to reduce ozone thinning?

■ Ozone thinning may be a problem for many decades. What are some of the ways you can protect yourself from the dangers posed by rising UV radiation?

THE James Bay PROJECT

by Burkhard Bilger

GETTING STARTED

- How important has energy become to modern society? What are the social and environmental costs of creating the energy you use?

- Is hydropower a good substitute for other sources of energy? If not, why not?

It has already displaced enough rock and soil to build the Great Pyramid of Cheops 80 times over and flooded an area the size of Lake Erie. It is one of the biggest feats of engineering ever undertaken on Earth. It's commonly called the James Bay Project and, unless you live in Canada, you may have never heard of it before now. If and when the James Bay Project is completed, it will generate enough electricity to supply much of Québec province, with enough left to export to the northeastern United States. Perhaps more importantly, the energy generated by James Bay will be as "clean" as energy gets. The project won't pollute the air, consume forests, or strip-mine landscapes. It will keep on producing electricity as long as rain falls and rivers flow.

James Bay may sound like the answer to a prayer—a clean source of power in an increasingly polluted world. But to John Petagumskum, the James Bay Project is a disaster. Petagumskum is a Cree Indian. He grew up on the shores of Hudson Bay, hunting and fishing in the forest as his people had done for countless generations. Today many of his people's sacred sites, camp locations, streams, and trapping runs rest far below the water's surface. They have been submerged beneath one of the lakes created by the James Bay Project's dams.

Energy is essential to your modern way of life. However, the electricity you use when you flip a light switch or boot up a computer must be produced and transported to you at some cost. In this case study, you will examine some of the costs, trade-offs, and difficult decisions involved in making electricity available.

CASE STUDY

AN APPETITE FOR ENERGY

Only a century ago, people had little need for projects such as James Bay. In those days, electricity was a luxury reserved for the rich living in a few large cities. Televisions, stereos, computers, camcorders, and all the other devices that are so much a part of your modern life had not yet been invented. In the late 1800s, heat came from burning coal or wood. Light came from candles or kerosene lamps. The energy required to do work was mostly provided by livestock or by the people themselves.

During the Industrial Revolution (late 1700s to mid-1800s), many craftsmen and small workshops were replaced by large facto-

2-1 There is a great deal of energy in running water and in the water that rushes over a waterfall. Iguazu Falls on the Argentina/Brazil border is a beautiful example. Massive hydropower plants, such as this one at LaGrande 2 in Québec, harness the power of moving water and turn it into electricity.

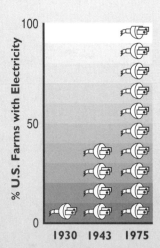

2-2 Electricity use has increased dramatically this century.

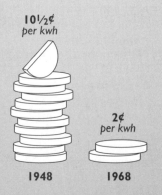

2-3 Increased use of electricity was spurred on by lower and lower costs.

2-4 Parts of a hydroelectric plant

ries and assembly lines. As tasks grew larger, one person's strength was no longer enough to do the work. The engines of mass production had to be fueled by escalating amounts of energy. Animal power and the energy derived from running water gave way to burning coal to make steam. Eventually industry began to turn to electricity for its energy needs.

By 1900, Europe, the United States, and Canada had become hooked on electricity. Cities were the first to be electrified, but the hunger for this convenient form of energy soon spread. As demand grew, utility companies found ways to produce electricity more efficiently, which in turn allowed them to lower the price. The more prices dropped, the more uses people found for electricity. Electric refrigerators, mixers, can openers, and toasters appeared in kitchens. Electric razors and hair dryers became common in bathrooms. Electricity was promoted as the energy of the future, and building contractors bragged about their new all-electric homes. Between 1963 and 1973, electricity consumption in the United States nearly doubled, and experts predicted that the use of electricity would continue to increase rapidly.

The Hydropower Solution?

The projections of Canada's energy needs were almost exactly the same as those for the United States. Faced with his own province's growing need for energy, Québec Premier Robert Bourassa decided

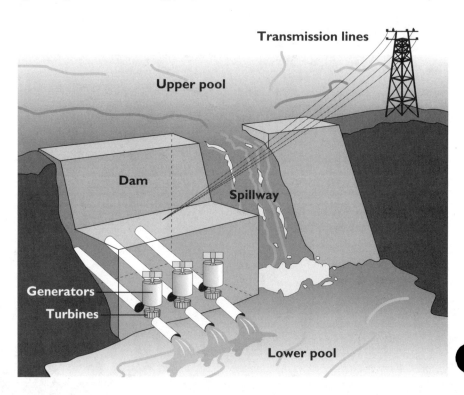

in 1971 to launch what he called "The Project of the Century." The James Bay hydropower project would harness the energy potential of northwestern Québec's rivers and rugged landscapes.

Hydropower is energy derived from running water. In a typical hydroelectric project, a river is dammed or diverted so that water is trapped in giant lakes or reservoirs. Once trapped, the water is gradually released through the dams, cascading over turbines. The water turns the blades of a turbine in the same way wind spins the blades of a toy propeller. The turning of the turbine blades spins the axle, which is attached to an electrical generator. As the axles of the huge generators are spun, electricity is produced. The electricity is then carried from the power plants to your kitchen or classroom through a series of cables, wires, and transformers.

Hydropower projects such as James Bay already provide about 25 percent of the world's electricity. More dams are being built every year. Between 1980 and 1985, 31 countries doubled their hydropower capacity. Brazil, with the world's largest dams, now gets 90 percent of its electricity from hydropower, as does the northwestern United States. However, one of the biggest disadvantages to hydropower is that, in more developed countries, most of the dam sites have already been used.

Hydropower has several advantages. It provides clean, renewable energy. A community that gets its electricity from hydropower does not need to build and maintain a power plant that burns fossil fuels or uses nuclear fuel. Another advantage to some hydropower is that the dams control flooding along rivers. The water stored in the reservoirs can sometimes be used for irrigating farms, for aquaculture, and for recreation.

The first phase of the James Bay Project (called the LaGrande Complex) was completed in 1984 and has a capacity of over 10 thousand megawatts— more than enough to cool and power a city the size of New York City on a sweltering July day. On the original schedule, the remaining phases of the James Bay Project (the Great Whale and Nottaway-Rupert-Broadback complexes) were to be completed by the year 2006. Those parts of the project would almost triple the total energy output. In this way, Québec hoped to meet its energy needs for the foreseeable future.

A LANDSCAPE UNDER WATER

However, this new source of energy has its costs— and the most obvious cost is the loss of valuable land. The enormous area affected by the James Bay Project has historically had relatively few human inhabitants. But those who live there— the Cree and Inuit Indians— live off the land itself. The area also contains one of North America's last pristine wildernesses. Moose, otter, bear, and

CONNECTIONS
EARTH SCIENCE

The rivers and streams that fill a reservoir with water usually carry sediment. Upon reaching the artificial base level of the reservoir, that sediment is dumped. In most areas, even the largest reservoirs can fill with sediment in only 100 to 200 years, ending the dam's usefulness in generating electricity.

2-5 Area of Québec affected by the James Bay Project

many other kinds of animals live in the affected region. Ducks and other birds feed in the coastal and riverside wetlands before migrating south. Trout swim in these rivers, and caribou—which outnumber people in the region 70 to 1—go there to have their young.

The James Bay Project is dramatically transforming the land. Already this hydropower project has diverted and backed-up major rivers in the Canadian province of Québec. By damming the local rivers, the project has created 27 new lakes and flooded tens of thousands of kilometers of riverbank. The people and animals who once lived in the affected area have had to move or adapt to the new conditions.

DISPLACING THE CREE

The Cree Indians have proved their ability to adjust to the eastern Canadian taiga forest. Archaeologists have shown that the Cree have lived in what is now Québec for over 6000 years. "We survived on the land and we did not leave a trace of our having been there," Grand Chief Matthew Coon-Come has said. "We did not construct great monuments or large earthworks. What we had and used came from the land and went back to the land. The land is sacred. It is a land of remembrance."

When the James Bay dams were first proposed in 1971, the Cree tribal council sent a letter to Canada's Minister of Indian Affairs,

CONNECTIONS
BIOLOGY
For more information on taiga forests, see the *Almanac* entry on page 79.

declaring: "We believe that only the beavers have the right to build dams on our territory." The Cree went to court to stop the James Bay Project. Although the Cree won an injunction halting construction, the court decision was reversed in 1974.

In 1975, after four years of bitter court battles, the Cree gave up their resistance to the LaGrande Complex. In a settlement with the Québec government and the Canadian national government, the Cree and the Inuit were awarded $225 million over 20 years. Also included in the settlement were a guaranteed income for each Cree and Inuit hunter who stayed in the wilderness for at least one third of the year, exclusive rights to trap, fish, and hunt nearly 75 000 square kilometers of land, training, and self-government.

However, there is a sense of unease among the Cree. The James Bay Project continues. The Cree have been left to rebuild lives that have for centuries been tied to a sense of *place*. With their land, the Cree may have also lost part of their culture. Many Cree have lost confidence in the land since the coming of the James Bay dams. A 1984 study showed that 64 percent of all Cree living in the village of Chisasibi had dangerous levels of mercury in their bodies. While some mercury may come from air polluting sources to the west, it seems that bacteria, feeding on the humus in soil submerged beneath the new James Bay reservoirs, had formed toxic methyl mercury. This toxic mercury entered the food chain, gradually building up in fish and then in the people who ate the fish. "The scientists come in here and tell us we're getting better," Cree fisherman George Lameboy told one reporter. "How can you measure a man's fear? How can you measure your way of life coming to an end?"

THE COSTS OF CHANGE

It is likely that many of the changes brought about by the James Bay Project will also have a negative effect on wildlife. If the Cree are having trouble adjusting to their displacement, what becomes of the caribou that migrated within the James Bay watershed? What happens to the fish and mussels that once thrived in the shallow, fast-running streams? Wetlands and spawning grounds have been drained or submerged, and beaver lodges have been washed away.

In one way, at least, the James Bay Project has even changed the effects of the seasons. Rivers usually carry nutrients to shoreline marshes and the bay year round. But society's demand for electricity does not match the seasonal supply of water. Hydropower reservoirs store water from spring and autumn rains and meltwater from the winter snows. In the United States, the greatest need for electricity is during the late summer when rainfall is at its lowest. In Canada, the greatest need for electricity is during the winter. ▶ Water is released through the dams during the drier months to produce electricity. Depriving the marshes and bays of the water and nutrients

CONNECTIONS
BIOLOGY

For more information on the food chain and ecosystems, see the *Almanac* entries on page 79.

Why is so much electricity consumed in the summer in the United States? Why would more electricity be used in the winter in Canada?

during the wet season may endanger the plants and animals that depend on this natural cycle.

No one knows exactly how such changes have or will affect the area in the long run. "In such a complex and fragile environment to which plants and wildlife have adapted successfully but precariously over the millennia," environmental journalist Peter Gorrie wrote in *Canadian Geographic*, "the impact could be catastrophic." The Cree believe that the court settlement with Québec and Canada only covered the first phase of the James Bay Project. The Cree and environmental groups, such as the Sierra Club, the James Bay Defense Coalition, and the Montreal-based Société pour Vaincre la Pollution (Society to Vanquish Pollution), are now lobbying to stop future dam-building in the area.

Not everyone agrees with this negative outlook. Hydro-Québec— the company in charge of the project— and many officials within the Québec government dismiss such reasoning. "Wildlife species inhabiting these areas are generally hardy pioneer species with wide ecological ranges," the company argues in its publication, *Future Hydro Development in Northern Québec: A Rational and Balanced Choice.* "They are adapted to highly variable living conditions and, as a result, their status was not jeopardized....The very presence of these species in the area is proof of their resistance."

> **FOCUS**
> Are these two sources stating facts or opinions? What information do you need to tell which side is right? How can that information be gathered?

WEIGHING THE PROS AND CONS

Clearly the James Bay Project's power comes at some cost. Is it worth it? Do less damaging sources of energy exist? As Hydro-Québec points out in one of its brochures: "It is essential...to put the risk and benefits of development into the overall energy supply perspective. The significance and the scale of the environmental impacts of different energy options must be weighed and compared." Remember that the James Bay Project produces an enormous amount of electricity. To produce as much electricity as the first phase of the James Bay Project alone, 28 nuclear or 60 coal- or oil-fired power plants would have to be built. So many nuclear plants would produce a large amount of radioactive waste and an ongoing risk of accidents and contamination. Coal and oil-burning power plants can add pollutants to the

> **FOCUS**
> What are the "costs" of the James Bay Project? Are these short-term or long-term costs? What are the benefits? Are those short-term or long-term?

air, which in turn can cause smog, acid rain, and respiratory illnesses. Perhaps worst of all, using such power plants to produce electricity would continue to deplete Earth's nonrenewable energy resources and contribute to the greenhouse effect.

By contrast, the costs of the first phase of the James Bay Project — the LaGrande Complex — have already been realized. The land and dams are paid for; the people and animals are adjusting to new conditions. Even the mercury levels in the reservoirs should return to normal within 20 to 30 years. More importantly, the James Bay hydroelectric plants will never stop producing clean, nonpolluting energy.

PROJECT ON HOLD

However, the LaGrande Complex is only the beginning of a much larger project. Opponents of James Bay argue that there's no need to complete the remaining phases of the project. They say that the project's additional electricity isn't necessary. North American demand for electricity abruptly leveled off in the 1970s. Tougher pollution controls and rising fossil fuel prices made the cost of producing electricity increase for the first time. Consumers, faced with higher monthly energy bills, made do with less electricity. Demand for electricity began to drop. Hydro-Québec, which predicted in the 1970s that energy consumption in Québec would grow by 7 percent every year, now says that it is growing by a little over 2 percent.

Demand for electricity could drop even more. Rising energy costs encourage conservation. During the 1980s, the average efficiency of new appliances in the United States rose by 10 to 20 percent. Appliances in Japan grew 50 percent more efficient over the same time period. Today, Swedish homes use between 30 and 50 percent less heat than similar-sized homes in the United States. According to one 1987 report, industrial countries could consume 2 percent less fossil fuel every year using only the existing technology. Air conditioners could be made more efficient by 40 percent, refrigerators and lighting by 75 percent. Critics of the James Bay Project argue that increasing energy efficiency in North America could— by itself— head off the need to build additional power plants of any kind.

Obviously if the need for energy decreased enough, there would be no need to complete the James Bay Project. Bill Namagoose, a spokesperson for the Cree, has said, "No culture should prosper and be enhanced at the expense of another. Conservation is the answer. With conservation, all cultures thrive." In a 1993 ad in *The New York Times*, a group of 42 Native American leaders voiced their opposition to James Bay and the idea of massive development projects.

> **CONNECTIONS**
> **BIOLOGY**
> For more information on acid rain, be sure to read Case Study 4 and the *Almanac* entry on page 79.

2-6 Switching from incandescent to fluorescent light bulbs can cut home electricity use in half.

Does the argument for conservation necessarily mean that the James Bay Project should be put on hold? Or should the project be completed as a replacement for the "dirtier" coal, oil, and nuclear-powered plants that currently produce the bulk of North America's electricity? ◀

NOTHING'S SIMPLE

Unfortunately, the more power is produced, the more it is used. For example, people living in the northwest United States, where hydropower produces electricity at nearly half the cost of elsewhere in the country, use twice as much energy as people in the rest of the country.

Québec has given mixed signals on moderating energy use. When the first James Bay power plants went on-line, the province encouraged aluminum smelters and other industries to relocate to Québec and buy the cheap surplus energy. This policy made sense: the government had an interest in providing jobs for the citizens of Québec. Price breaks and ad campaigns encouraged the Québecois (the people of Québec) to consume more electricity rather than less. With nearly $15 billion invested in just the first phase of the James Bay Project, the province was scrambling to recoup its investment. More recently the government has been encouraging conservation.

There may also be political motives for the province of Québec to continue and finish the James Bay Project. From the time Canada was granted the status of a self-governing state within the British Empire in 1867, the French-speaking Canadians have desired greater freedom from the national government. (Canada was finally granted full independence from Great Britain in 1987.) Since the 1960s, Québec has pursued a course that they hope will lead them to the formation of a separate nation. Having industries in place, ample jobs, and a source of abundant energy for sale and use, all make Québec's secession from Canada an easier step to take. It may take years before Québec can fully concentrate on conservation and truly realize an environmental benefit from James Bay's hydroelectric power.

> **FOCUS** ▶
>
> If the technology to use less electricity is available, why hasn't it been used? What economic or political reasons could states or communities in the U.S. have for remaining relatively energy inefficient or for not developing alternative energy, such as solar and wind power?

ANALYSIS

IDENTIFY THE PROBLEM
- List the costs and benefits of the James Bay Project. Prioritize the items on each list and determine which costs and benefits are long-term and which are short-term.
- Which individuals, groups, or agencies are on each of the two sides in the James Bay debate? How do their reasons for opposing or supporting the project differ?
- What information still needs to be gathered to judge the project's effect on the environment and on society?

LOOKING MORE CLOSELY: ISSUES
- Assume for a minute that completing the James Bay Project is in the best economic and political interests of Québec as a whole. Should these interests supersede the interests of the Cree Indians? Explain.

SCIENCE TAKING SIDES
- Supporters of hydropower say that it prevents additional burning of coal, which releases carbon dioxide, a greenhouse gas. Opponents of the James Bay Project say that the soil and rotting wood submerged in the reservoirs is releasing just as much greenhouse gas as a coal-fired plant and that hydropower is not so "clean" after all. Explain the flaws you see in both positions.

PLOTTING THE FUTURE
- Using the data on page 80 of the *Almanac*, graph world production of oil, the amount of electricity from nuclear power plants. What do these graphs tell you?
- Based on the data on page 80, how many Canadian, Sri Lankan, Tunisian, French, Guatemalan, or Japanese citizens, would it take to consume as much energy as one United States citizen?

ACTING ON THE ISSUE

ENERGY AND YOUR COMMUNITY
- Research where and how your community's electricity is generated.
- Are there sources of energy available to your community that are more environmentally friendly than those currently in use?
- What could your community do to become more energy efficient?
- Would these measures cost or save your community money in the short- and long-term? What possible things stand in the way of these measures being adopted?

A Burning Question

by Robert F. Ehrhardt

GETTING STARTED

- Where do hazardous wastes originate? What are the problems with hazardous wastes?
- Is incineration a good alternative for disposing of hazardous wastes? If not, why not?

Love Canal. Valley of a Thousand Drums. These names echo through the environmental history books — sad testaments to waste management gone wrong. Industry generates millions of tons of hazardous wastes a year. These wastes must be disposed of in a way that won't harm or threaten the environment. After all, some of these substances can kill people, other animals, or plants upon contact. Other substances take longer to do their damage. They can slowly attack the nervous system, cause cancer, or lead to birth defects. This is the type of damage discovered at New York State's Love Canal in the 1970s.

You might say it would be possible to avoid all harm from hazardous wastes by simply not producing them. However, hazardous wastes are by-products of life in an industrialized society. The manufacture of things people use in their daily lives — clothing that doesn't wrinkle, the plastics in cars and compact discs, cutting-edge medicines — contributes to the hazardous waste problem. The wastes are generated while these products are being made. Until it's possible to produce materials without forming hazardous wastes, there needs to be a way to dispose of the wastes safely.

In this case study, you will examine a controversy surrounding one method of hazardous waste disposal — waste incinerators. With strict air pollution controls and well-trained personnel, incineration can be the safest method of disposal for most types of hazardous wastes. Yet some people think that incineration carries with it a potential threat to public health and the environment. How does a town balance the possible health risks from having a hazardous waste incinerator nearby against what some see as the town's economic survival? There are no easy answers. Welcome to East Liverpool, Ohio.

CASE STUDY

AN INCINERATOR FOR EAST LIVERPOOL

East Liverpool, Ohio, is a small town located about 30 miles northwest of Pittsburgh, Pennsylvania. Emigrants from England came to East Liverpool in the 1800s, drawn by reports of the nearby natural clay deposits. East Liverpool became known as "The Pottery

3-1 Hazardous wastes are dangerous when discarded improperly. Burning wastes in specially designed incinerators, such as the one in East Liverpool, is one option for proper disposal.

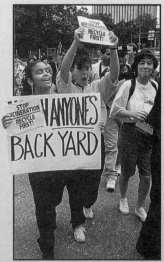

3-2 People protesting the operation of a hazardous waste incinerator.

When are the economic benefits of an action more important than the risk of harm to the environment?

Capital of America." At its peak, East Liverpool was surrounded by pottery kilns, steel mills, and other heavy industries. However, the once-important pottery and steel companies have gone out of business. With fewer jobs available, people moved away. Today East Liverpool has only half the population it had in its boom years.

Like any town falling on hard times, the town officials of East Liverpool were eager to secure new jobs and income for their citizens. In 1981, a company called Waste Technologies Inc. (WTI) decided to build and operate a hazardous waste incinerator in East Liverpool. The town officials approved the incinerator. Many people in East Liverpool looked forward to the change in the local economy. "It's been 50 years since a major industry has moved to East Liverpool, " says Michael Parkes of the local Chamber of Commerce. "Having a new industry come here is unheard of."

Building the incinerator has been easier than using it. The incinerator is the seventh largest in the country. Construction on the incinerator was completed in 1992. However, since the plans for the incinerator were annnounced in 1981, the incinerator has been a center of controversy.

THE LESSER OF TWO EVILS

The East Liverpool incinerator controversy revolves around possible health risks and the potential threat to the local environment. ◄ While town officials at first thought that health risks from the incinerator would be minimal, some East Liverpool citizens did not. Those people who feared the risks of living near the incinerator took the matter to court and held protest rallies. Already these protests have delayed the plant's opening.

Not everyone fears the incinerator. Some people are quick to point out the benefits of incineration. East Liverpool resident Denny Brennan says he favors the incinerator. He feels that the incinerator is an environmentally sound way to dispose of hazardous wastes. "This installation is safe. Where [else] are you going to dump that stuff? It's got to go somewhere. I can show you places where the sides of a hill are covered with dumped chemicals," Brennan says.

The Environmental Protection Agency (EPA) estimates that the United States produces at least 240 million metric tons of hazardous wastes each year. Industry is by far the largest source, generating waste as it manufactures the products people expect to use in their everyday lives. The EPA definition of hazardous wastes does not include waste produced by hospitals, small businesses, and households. Nonetheless, paint, oven cleaner, and motor oil are considered hazardous waste when it comes time to throw them away. They too must be disposed of carefully.

HARD TO HANDLE

In the past, hazardous wastes were commonly dumped on the land, buried in the ground, injected into deep wells, or dumped into the ocean. Sometimes organic chemicals compounds, biological wastes, and flammable materials were incinerated.

Each of these disposal methods is a potential threat to public health and to the environment. When hazardous wastes are dumped onto the ground or injected into deep wells, the waste may move into groundwater, poisoning water supplies. Buried containers may leak hazardous wastes contaminating soil and water. When hazardous wastes are burned in open fires — or in incinerators that don't have proper pollution controls — the emissions pollute the air.

The EPA has hundreds of documented cases on file describing damage from the improper management of hazardous wastes. The towns of Toone and Teague, Tennessee, are examples. Their water supplies were contaminated with organic compounds when water leached from a nearby landfill. When the landfill closed, it held some 350 000 drums filled with hazardous wastes. Many of the drums were leaking pesticide-related wastes. Today the two towns no longer have local access to uncontaminated groundwater.

Proper waste management means more than just careful disposal. It also means consideration of other options. A small percentage of hazardous wastes are stored in EPA-approved, secured landfills. These are specially designed landfills that are continually monitored.

A smaller percentage of hazardous wastes are currently being incinerated. Modern incinerators aren't anything like the smoke-belching, air-polluting ovens of a hundred years ago. Today's hazardous waste incinerators are sophisticated, high-tech facilities. They are clean and computer-

CONNECTIONS
CHEMISTRY

For more information on organic chemical compounds, see the *Almanac* entry on page 81.

CONNECTIONS
ENVIRONMENT

The federal government program for hazardous waste clean-up is called the Superfund. For information on the Superfund, see the *Almanac* entry on page 81.

The **AFTERBURNER** destroys organic chemicals released during the initial burn.

The **SPRAY DRYER** cools the offgas to 230°C. All liquids are removed.

The **ELECTROSTATIC PRECIPITATOR** removes 99% of particulate matter greater than 1 μm in diameter.

The **KILN** exposes hazardous waste to temperatures ranging from 650°C–1150°C.

Toxic ash is collected and prepared for disposal.

Ash disposal → **LANDFILL**

CONNECTIONS
CHEMISTRY

For more information on hazardous wastes, see the *Almanac* entry on page 81.

FOCUS

Do people think about all the risks they actually face in their life every day? Why do people decide to focus on some risks and not others?

controlled and have many safety systems. Incineration destroys organic hazardous substances and reduces waste volume. The remaining ash, which contains toxic metals, is then deposited in a hazardous waste site.

Too Close for Comfort

People who live close to a modern hazardous waste incinerator may worry about what is released into the air from the stacks. The people understand that the emissions can contain toxic chemicals that can be health hazards. Because the pollution is in the air they breathe, people may be exposed to chemicals in their homes, schools, and workplaces. Excessive exposure to these toxic chemicals could lead to birth defects and an increased risk of cancer.

How much of an airborne pollutant is "too much"? The EPA and other public and private researchers study the dangers of incinerator emissions. These long-term studies report the risk of cancer from incinerator emissions to be no greater than 1 person in 100 000. According to the EPA, this is an "acceptable risk."

However, many members of the public believe there is no such thing as an acceptable risk. They think that if you are exposed to *any* cancer-causing chemicals you are at risk. ◀ According to their position, if you are exposed to even one toxic molecule, you could get cancer sometime during your life.

WTI argues that the plant in East Liverpool will have little impact on the environment. "We are the best, the safest, the newest," says WTI spokesperson Julia Bircher. The incinerator has been redesigned several times during the last twelve years. WTI has used the latest incinerator and pollution control technologies. The

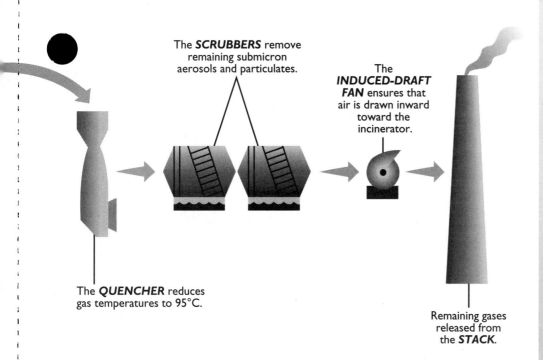

3-3 Parts of a hazardous waste incinerator.

company claims that its incinerator safely destroys 99.99 percent of the waste put into it. WTI also says that the plant's air pollution control system will eliminate nearly everything from its air emissions except for water vapor and carbon dioxide.

A Town Divided

It's the "nearly everything" that has some citizens and environmental groups worried. Citizens opposed to the incinerator say that — even by WTI's reasoning — the incinerator will release cancer-causing chemicals into the air. The incinerator has the capability of burning approximately 80 000 tons of hazardous waste per year. If 99.99 percent of that waste is destroyed, several tons of pollutants may still go up the stacks. Opponents to the incinerator point out that people who live in nearby homes, will breathe these pollutants. Some town residents feel that emissions from the incinerator will be deposited in water supplies and on food crops in the region.

Other residents, while less than enthusiastic about the incinerator, still think it should be allowed to operate. Sue Jackson points to the existing risks from chemicals moving through the area by rail, truck, and river barge. "Look at what comes [through] here every day. You pretty much got it any way you go." Others say that they support operating the incinerator as long as the emissions are closely monitored. Some citizens are looking at the economic consequences. If the incinerator never opens, the town will lose millions of dollars each year in payrolls and in local taxes.

The incinerator debate has disrupted friendships and families throughout East Liverpool. Sandy Estell lives in a neighborhood next to the incinerator. She says, "There are so many bad feelings,

CONNECTIONS
BIOLOGY

Little is understood about how the interaction between living cells and environmental factors such as radiation or certain chemicals causes cancer. However, scientists think up to 10 % of known cancers are caused by environmental factors.

FOCUS

How might an individual's personal history or present economic condition affect her or his opinion?

it's going to be hard to put all this behind us." Video store owner Vern Shafer Jr. says, "This town basically has been destroyed. People who were friends for 50 years won't even talk to each other, just because of a stand taken over WTI."

STANDING IDLE

The controversy in East Liverpool reveals some important questions about hazardous waste disposal. Why shouldn't the East Liverpool incinerator be allowed to open? WTI says that it is losing over $100 000 every day that the incinerator is not permitted to operate. WTI argues that it has satisfied all government requirements regarding safe operations and installation of pollution-control equipment. In April 1993, the EPA approved limited operation of the incinerator after WTI completed a trial burn. However, additional data later led to the EPA placing further restrictions on how much waste the plant could safely burn. This reopened discussions about the incinerator's safety. The incinerator will bring jobs and tax revenues to a town in great need of both. Perhaps most importantly, the incinerator will destroy dangerous hazardous wastes that would otherwise have to be destroyed or stored elsewhere.

Hazardous wastes continue to be generated every day. As this country runs out of acceptable landfills, incineration becomes a more attractive alternative. On the other hand, people have concerns about the health risks from having such an incinerator in their state. As East Liverpool waits for a decision about its incinerator dilemma, the rest of the country should focus on the broader question: What should be done with hazardous wastes?

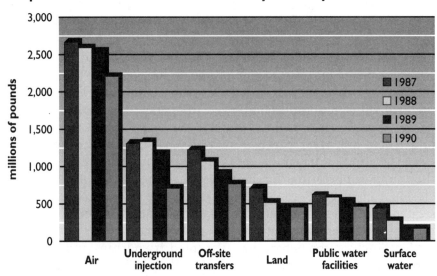

3-4 Efforts are being made to reduce hazardous waste. Yet, disposal continues to be a problem.

ANALYSIS

IDENTIFY THE PROBLEM
- What are the arguments for and against opening the East Liverpool incinerator?
- Would you oppose locating a hazardous waste incinerator in your community? Explain your answer. If you oppose incineration, how would you propose that the hazardous waste generated in your community and state be managed?
- Scientists for the EPA state that the risk of getting cancer from hazardous waste incinerator emissions is 1 person in 100 000. By comparison, the risk of getting cancer from industrial emissions and car exhaust in the Los Angeles area is 1 additional cancer in 1000 persons. Is 1 in 100 000 an "acceptable risk"? Who, or what group, do you think should decide what is an "acceptable risk"?

LOOKING MORE CLOSELY: ISSUES
- Debate the following statement: Cities and companies in the United States should ship large amounts of hazardous wastes to other countries.

LOOKING MORE CLOSELY: SCIENCE
- Examine the incinerator diagram (Figure 3-3). What becomes of ash from hazardous waste incineration? Is ash from hazardous waste incineration also hazardous?

ACTING ON THE ISSUES

HAZARDS IN YOUR BACKYARD
- Find out what hazardous wastes are generated at your school and in your home. What happens to these wastes?
- Contact the agency that regulates hazardous wastes in your state and ask for a list of known hazardous waste disposal sites. Check with the EPA to see if there is a federal site listed in your area.
- Create a list of "environmentally-friendly" products that can be used as alternatives to some of the hazardous products found in your home.
- Contact your local health department or environmental agency for information on what to do with hazardous chemicals found in your home or your school. Is there a "hazardous waste day" in your town? What wastes are collected? Where are they disposed?

Acid on the Wind

by Burkhard Bilger

GETTING STARTED

- How do changes in one element of an ecosystem influence other elements of the system?
- How would reducing acid rain benefit the people of the United States? The people of the world?
- Who should pay to reduce acid rain?
- Is reducing acid rain too expensive?

CONNECTIONS
EARTH SCIENCE

For more information on the water cycle, see the *Almanac* entry on page 87.

Long before anyone had heard the phrases "air pollution" and "Earth Day," the people of New York State decided to preserve the Adirondacks for future generations. The oldest mountains in North America, the Adirondacks, were weathered and worn by the time the ancestors of the Iroquois arrived. The lakes teemed with brook trout and bass, and the pine, hemlock, and spruce forests were alive with game. From the top of Mt. Marcy, known to the local Native Americans as Tahawus or "Cloud Splitter," a trapper's eye could run from peak to peak of unspoiled country.

New Yorkers created the Adirondack Park in 1892 and in their state's constitution declared that the park's lands would stay "forever wild." Over the years, they expanded the park until it grew to 6 million acres of public and private land — the largest park in the country outside of Alaska.

For decades, people came to the Adirondacks to enjoy the wilderness. They came for quiet and solitude or to cast their fishing lines into the rushing brooks and quiet lakes. But then something began to go wrong. "Just when it seemed we had achieved a proper balance of preservation and development — the scourge of acid rain began to evidence itself in the form of dead lakes." These words were written in an open letter to Congress in 1987 by the Adirondack Council, a nonprofit group formed to protect the park. The Adirondacks, one of the country's most treasured areas, were suddenly a potential environmental disaster.

Acid rain is a by-product of an industrialized society. Everyone would like to see it go away, but getting rid of acid rain has a price tag. Is the price tag too high? Can industry afford to pay to keep the Adirondacks forever wild and still remain competitive? Here is a dilemma with no easy answers.

CASE STUDY

FINDING THE SOURCE

Rainwater is the lifeblood of the Adirondacks. Now the water that courses through the mountain streams, rivers, and lakes is often acidic enough to dissolve copper and lead from pipes and plumbing joints. How has this happened? New Yorkers had to look for the

4-1 Vacationland and getaway for people, habitat for many plants and animals, this wilderness country is threatened by pollutants released into the atmosphere.

4-2 The major sources of acid rain pollutants (black dots).

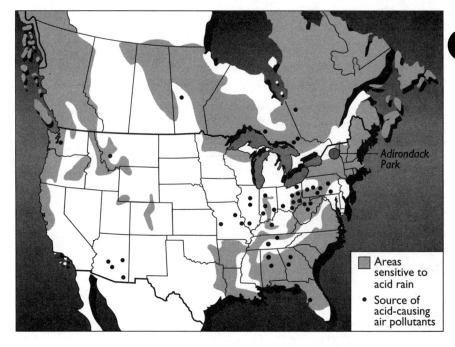

FOCUS
Are there disadvantages to burning more oil? What problems are there in the use of nuclear power?

source of acid rain outside of their state as well as within it. They backtracked west along the prevailing winds, beyond the Appalachians, across a time zone and a third of the country to the industrial areas of Ohio, Indiana, and Illinois. There they found a possible source of the acid rain. Coal-burning power plants and factories were releasing millions of tons of smoke into the air. To protect their local cities from pollution, many midwest industries had built smokestacks tall enough for its smoke to be swept away by the winds. The peaks of the Adirondacks, as it happens, are in the direct path of these winds. The tons of emissions from midwest smokestacks are thought by many experts to be the source of nearly half of the acid in the Adirondacks' rain.

Should industries in Ohio be required to protect the distant Adirondacks? The Clean Air Act of 1990 says yes. It requires that smokestack industries find a way to reduce acid-making emissions. One option is for industries to convert from coal to more expensive fuels such as oil, gas, or nuclear power. However, converting factories to these cleaner fuels would have a healthy price tag. In addition, the cost of producing goods would go up.

A company could also decide to continue to burn coal but to do it cleanly. This can be done by fitting smokestacks with special equipment called scrubbers that removes acid-producing emissions. But these scrubbers and other efficient combustion equipment are expensive to buy. They also increase operating costs by as much as 15 percent. The added investment and the higher production costs would be passed on in higher prices to the consumer. If prices for goods go up, economists wonder whether United States industries can continue to compete with foreign manufacturers. Many foreign countries don't require their manufacturers to meet pollution standards equal to those of the Clean Air Act. If industries in the United States can't compete, factories will close and jobs will be lost. On the other hand, many environmentalists and economists alike argue that protecting the environment will create new jobs by stimulating research into new, clean technologies.

Moving away from coal would also hurt the coal-mining industry. In the past, every conversion of an industry from coal to a cleaner fuel has cost coal miners' their jobs. Ask the factory workers of the midwest and the miners of West Virginia if they care about harming the Adirondacks and you'll hear a definite yes. However, they will be quick to add that they care more about keeping their jobs and being able to support their families. They know that if pollution controls are too costly, their industry or mining company could close. These are troubling issues to balance against the ideal of an unspoiled environment.

CONNECTIONS ECONOMICS
Another option for power companies is to trade in pollution credits. For more information, see the *Almanac* entry on page 82.

HOW RAIN BECOMES ACID

Acid rain falling on the lakes, streams, and forests of the Adirondacks is completing a long, tortuous trek. The journey begins in the coal mines of Tennessee, Kentucky, and West Virginia, and in oil fields throughout the world. Fossil fuels containing acid-making substances are removed from these areas, refined, and carried to gas tanks and furnaces throughout the country.  There they are burned to power cars, run factories, smelt metals, and generate electricity. Coal contains varying amounts of sulfur which, when burned, combines with oxygen to create sulfur dioxide. Oxides of nitrogen are formed when fuel oil and gasoline are burned. Sulfur dioxide is responsible for about two thirds of the acid in acid rain, while oxides of nitrogen account for the other third.

Ironically acid rain is a result of processes that wash the atmosphere clean of pollutants found in factory smoke and automobile exhaust. These pollutants — sulfur dioxide and nitrogen oxides — travel with the winds. Other gases in the atmosphere react with them to create sulfuric acid and nitric acid. These acids combine with water droplets in clouds and are flushed to Earth as acid rain. Acid droplets also fall to the ground on their own.

FOCUS
How were coal and oil created? Why are they called fossil fuels? What are the environmental costs of extracting them?

ACID RAIN HARMS AQUATIC ANIMALS

In 1987, the Adirondack Council reported that more than 26 percent of Adirondack lakes and ponds were "critically acidified." These lakes had pH values below 5.0. The report predicted that another 20 percent of the region's lakes and ponds would become critically acidified if acid rain continued at 1987 levels.

What happens to the animals that live in those lakes and ponds? Some species can tolerate acids better than others. Frogs, for instance, get along all right in water with a pH as low as 4.0, while clams and snails need a pH of 6.0 or higher. The most prized sport

CONNECTIONS CHEMISTRY
For more information on pH, see the *Almanac* entry on page 82.

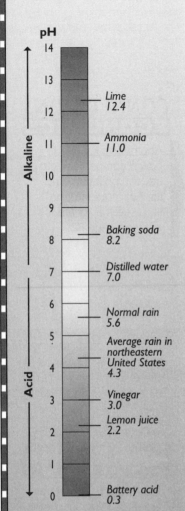

4-3 Scale of pH, used to measure acidity and alkalinity of water solutions.

CONNECTIONS
BIOLOGY

For more information on food chains see the *Almanac* entry on page 79.

fish — the brook trout — has one of the lowest tolerances for acidity. The brook trout population is thought to be declining throughout the Adirondacks. Of course, even species that thrive in acid water can die out when the plants or animals they eat don't share their tolerance for higher acidity. According to the United States Environmental Protection Agency, lakes in the Adirondack, Pocono, and Catskill mountains may already have lost 69 percent of their leeches, 50 percent of their snails and freshwater clams, and 45 percent of their insects. These statistics show that ecosystems are collapsing.

Many species of aquatic animals are particularly threatened in early spring when acids, locked up in winter snow, are suddenly released as the snow melts. Highly acidic runoff pours into the shallow lakes and ponds just as fish eggs and insect larvae are ready to hatch. The sudden increase in acidity keeps some species from reproducing.

Forest Devastation

Stands of red spruce at elevations over 800 meters have been ravaged by acid rain over the last half century. Damage to sugar maples has also raised concern. Acid rain attacks trees by taking nutrients from the leaves and the surrounding soil. The acid frees aluminum atoms from the soil in which they are bound, making it possible for the aluminum to poison tree roots. Acids also encourage damaging mosses to grow around tree trunks.

However, acid rain may not be the only thing damaging the forests. Many scientists think that they can prove acid rain is damaging high-altitude spruce forest. But other damage may be due to such things as drought, severe winter cold, insect infestations, and rising levels of ozone in Earth's lower atmosphere. Other very long-term natural processes may be at work, but it's hard for short-term scientific studies to prove that they are taking place.

Adirondack Sensitivity

Not all scientists agree on how acidic the Adirondack lakes have become nor how badly the Adirondack forests have been damaged.

Two groups of scientists using different methods to measure the effects of acid rain came up with different conclusions. Both groups agree that the Adirondacks have been harmed by acid rain, but one group speculates that the region may have natural geologic features that make it particularly vulnerable. For example, Adirondack lakes don't neutralize acids well because the principal rock that underlies the region is granite. Granitic rocks and the soils that form from them can't neutralize acid as well as the limestone rocks and soils that surround lakes in other regions.

Scientists have learned that microbes living in the sediments on lake bottoms can neutralize acid, but they need five years to do so. Unfortunately, water rushes through Adirondack lakes and streams far faster than it does through many healthy midwestern lakes — too fast for microbes to neutralize acid significantly.

4-4 Research has shown that fish and other aquatic organisms are sensitive to changes in acid levels.

The Clean Air Act

Acid rain is not a local issue. Pollution not only travels from state to state but also crosses national borders. For example, many Canadians contend that much of the acid rain affecting Canada's forestry and fishing-related tourist industries comes from the United States. ▶

Should the United States be responsible for damage to Canadian forests and the tourist industry?

The United States took the first step toward halting acid rain by passing the Clean Air Act in 1970. The act set limits on air pollution that helped to reduce sulfur dioxide emissions by a third over the next twenty years. Nevertheless, reports of damage caused by acid rain continued to flow in over that same period. These reports made it clear that the pollution standards in the Clean Air Act needed stiffening. In November 1990, amendments to the Clean Air Act were passed that specifically target acid rain. The new act says that by the year 2000, sulfur dioxide emission levels should be no more than half the levels of emissions recorded in 1980. Emissions of nitrogen oxides are to be cut by 10 percent each year.

The 1990 Clean Air Act offers some hope to the Adirondacks. According to the National Acid Precipitation Assessment Program, the Act's provisions should allow most Adirondack lakes to support fish by the year 2010.

Who Should Pay?

Controversy swirls around the acid rain issue. Some economists feel that the Clean Air Act goes too far. They think that power companies and smokestack industries should not bear the entire

FOCUS

What effect would the introduction of these changes in the auto industry have on the oil industry?

burden of cleaning the air. ◄ According to the scientific data, they say, it's not clear where the responsibility lies. There are other sources of acid rain.

Automobile exhaust is one of these sources. Efforts to improve the efficiency of automobile engines have not yet been sufficient to reduce the level of auto exhaust air pollutants significantly. If the average gas mileage of automobiles was increased by one third, the amount of gasoline burned each day on the road would decrease by 25 percent, resulting in a 25 percent reduction in auto exhaust. Highly efficient gasoline engines have already been built. Engines that use clean-burning alternative fuels are also realistic options. Some alternative-fuel cars, built by innovative new companies, are already in use in a few places, but they are very expensive.

LOOKING FOR ANSWERS

The red spruce on the summits of Adirondack peaks are slowly dying. Even though acid-tolerant balsam firs are taking their places, the forest will never be the same. The spruce are a symbol of possibly irreversible changes in a sensitive environment. What will happen in the future in other regions that now seem healthy and unaffected by acid rain?

Industry will grow as population grows and with it the potential for greater acid-making pollution. Increased population means more automobiles on the road. Power companies and manufacturers are concerned about costs and their ability to remain profitable. Factory workers and miners worry about their jobs. Consumers don't want to pay higher prices.

At the same time, no one wants to lose places like Adirondack Park. People want to go there and cast their lines in streams with abundant fish. They want to enjoy the outdoors and reconnect with the natural world. As increased population strains the limited parks and recreational areas of Earth, preservation of such places will hinge upon decisions made today.

4-5 Industry has been researching the development of small, more fuel efficient cars. However car manufacturers are reluctant to invest in them.

ANALYSIS

IDENTIFY THE PROBLEM
- What are the effects of acid rain on the forests and the animal systems of the Adirondacks?
- How do people benefit when a natural environment is preserved? What costs may the public need to bear to preserve places like Adirondack Park?
- What obligations may the developed nations of the world have toward underdeveloped nations as they begin to industrialize? List reasons why acid rain should be treated as a global problem.

PLOTTING THE FUTURE
- Using the data in the tables on page 82 of the *Almanac*, graph sulfur dioxide emissions in Germany, the United Kingdom, and the United States from 1970 to 1989. In which country did emissions drop the fastest? Create a similar graph of nitrogen emissions in those countries. What conclusions can you draw from these graphs?

LOOKING MORE CLOSELY: ISSUES
- According to the data on page 83 of the *Almanac*, where are populations rising faster — in industrialized or in developing countries? Industrialized countries like the United States are currently responsible for almost all emissions of sulfur dioxide and oxides of nitrogen. How may that change over the next 30 years? How will that change affect the United States? Controlling industrial air pollution requires expensive, sophisticated technology. How can the United States best help developing countries keep their emissions down?

ACTING ON THE ISSUES

LOOKING FOR ACIDITY
- Research which industries in your area emit sulfur dioxide and oxides of nitrogen. How many tons do they emit every year? Do they have air pollution control devices?
- Use a map of the country's prevailing winds to find out where the pollution over your state may come from or where it may go.
- Test the pH of your local rainfall. Is it more acidic than natural rainwater? If so, how many times more acidic?

Something in the Water

by Gloria J. Dyer

GETTING STARTED

- How does groundwater become polluted? Why can't groundwater cleanse itself effectively?
- Why would groundwater pollution controls be opposed?

It's late morning and the fire fighters are just starting to roll up their water hoses, stow their ladders, and pack the trucks to leave. The air smells of the fire — and something else, something that smells of both smoke and paint thinner. People had been able to see the flames from this fire for miles around. The thick, black smoke filled the sky. Now all that's left is the wet, charred remains of the warehouse and the water draining out the back and into the nearby field. You would never know that the *real* disaster has only just begun.

On the other side of the country, a farmer watches as the biplane dives out of the dawn sky and down toward his grapevines. As the plane levels off close to the ground, it releases a cloud of yellow pesticide and then pulls up, climbing back into the air. The farmer is having his fields sprayed to control a nasty fungus that is attacking his vines. The pesticide settles to the ground. Some of it coats the grapevines where it begins to attack the fungus. The rest covers the soil between the vines. It will still be there when the farmer irrigates on the weekend. The water will carry the pesticide deep into the soil. After that, the pesticide will be gone forever — or will it be gone at all?

A surprising amount of drinking water in the United States comes from groundwater — the water found beneath Earth's surface. That groundwater is under increasing threats of being permanently polluted by a number of sources. In both of the situations above, the groundwater has been contaminated. What seemed harmless at the time later turned out to be an environmental nightmare. In this case study, you will see how two different kinds of groundwater pollution have affected drinking water in two different parts of the country. Can groundwater continue to be a plentiful source of clean water — or is there poison in the well?

CASE STUDY

PRECIOUS COMMODITY

You may think that the last thing that would be in short supply on this planet would be water. Observed from space, Earth seems to be almost covered with blue liquid. But even though water covers 71

5-1 Some of California's most fertile farmlands are irrigated by water taken from below Earth's surface. That same water is used to supply drinking water. What happens when pollutants enter that water supply?

43

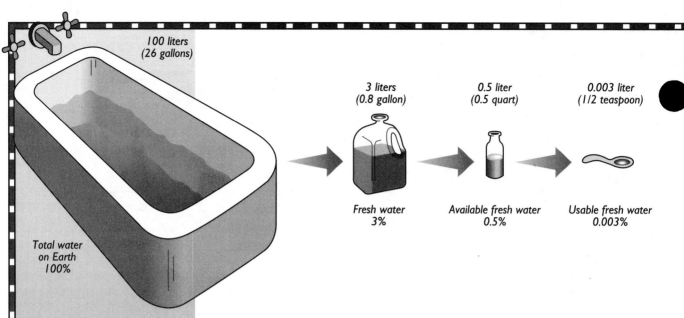

5-2 Very little of Earth's water is usable fresh water.

CONNECTIONS
EARTH SCIENCE

For more information on the water cycle, see the *Almanac* entry on page 87.

CONNECTIONS
EARTH SCIENCE

About 97 percent of Earth's liquid fresh water is groundwater. For more information on groundwater and aquifers, see the *Almanac* entry on page 84.

percent of Earth's surface, 97 percent of that water is in the form of the salt water in the oceans.

Life depends on fresh water. Unfortunately, most of Earth's fresh water is unusable. Much of it is frozen in the ice caps and other glaciers. Some of it is stored in the pore spaces of soil and rock — sometimes so deep underground that it isn't practical to pump it out. Only 0.003 percent of Earth's water is liquid, fresh, and readily available for use by life on land.

Water is continually moving through the water cycle. Yet, even though the water cycle forms fresh water, sometimes there isn't enough fresh water for people to use. In the United States, the problem is not so much that there isn't enough fresh water, but that it isn't always in the right place at the right time. Over 75 percent of the United States population lives on only 2 percent of the land. Such concentrated populations — and the water-using industries that go with them — put tremendous demands on the nearby sources of fresh water. Cities look to any fresh water source to supply needed drinking water for their citizens and water for industry. Some cities, such as New York City and Los Angeles, bring water in through huge aqueducts from sources hundreds of kilometers away. Other cities drill wells and pump fresh groundwater from beneath Earth's surface.

THE WATER BELOW

Groundwater has become a very important — and perhaps overused — source of fresh water. In the United States, groundwater provides 35 percent of the public water supply and 40 percent of the water used for the irrigation of agricultural crops.

Many people buy bottled "spring water" because they assume that groundwater is purer than drinking water that comes out of a faucet. Yet groundwater can become polluted. Pesticides, sewage from home septic systems, gasoline leaking from underground storage tanks, and water leaching through landfills can all find their way into the supposedly clean water supply. Unfortunately, once the pollutants are in the groundwater, it is difficult to get them out.

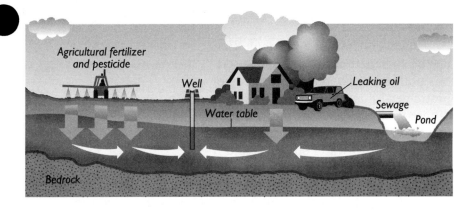

5-3 How many different pollutants might be found in water from this well?

Unlike water at Earth's surface, groundwater does not easily rid itself of pollutants.

For decades, people assumed that any chemicals used in the air or in the soil would break down and become harmless before they could ever reach the groundwater. The first discovery of tiny amounts of pesticides in 2500 California wells in 1979 showed that this assumption was false. The manufacturers had claimed that their pesticides were harmless in the concentrations commonly used. However, it was later discovered that some pesticides — such as the now-banned DDT — build up in the food chain, poisoning higher level consumers.

It is difficult to tell when water is contaminated because many contaminants are as odorless and colorless as water itself. Discovering contamination in groundwater is even more difficult because the water is hidden beneath Earth's surface.

At the opening of a United States Congressional hearing on groundwater contamination in 1989, Congressman John Hiler of Indiana spoke of the need for greater attention to the nation's groundwater. He called groundwater contamination "one of the most significant, most important problems the country faces." Hiler's strong opinion was backed up by evidence from across the country. A 1984 study found that 63 percent of rural Americans may be drinking water that has excessive levels of pesticides and other contaminants. In 1988, the Environmental Protection Agency (EPA) reported finding 46 different pesticides in the groundwater of 26 states.

THE PRICE OF PESTS

Many people believe that the benefits of using pesticides outweigh the possible risks. Pesticides are used to save lives by controlling insect-carried diseases such as malaria and typhus. Pesticides prevent agricultural pests from destroying crops, leading to greater production and lower food costs to the consumer. Even with the use of pesticides, over half the world's potential food supply is lost to pests either before or after harvesting. Without pesticides, food supplies would dwindle and prices would rise.

CONNECTIONS
BIOLOGY

For more information on how toxins accumulate in the food chain, see the *Almanac* entry on page 79.

CONNECTIONS
BIOLOGY

Pesticides are chemicals that are used to kill or control a pest. A pest may be an insect, a weed, a rodent, a worm, a fungus, or some other organism that harms humans, livestock, or crops.

However, the same pesticide that can be so beneficial also can be a serious pollutant. There are hundreds of pesticides in use and all of them have different chemical formulas. No one knows which pesticides currently pose a threat to water supplies, and it is also difficult to pinpoint the exact sources of contamination. However, the amount of pesticides in use is staggering. Although some states and countries use more pesticides than others, the average amount used in 1990 was about half a kilogram per year for every person living on Earth.

Agriculture is not the only source of pesticides contaminating the groundwater. Many people use pesticides on their lawns and in their homes. Other pesticides are used in building materials. But the greatest quantities of pesticides are used in agriculture.

Groundwater (and surface water) contaminated with pesticides presents a serious health threat. A 1987 EPA study estimated that in the United States up to 20 000 cases of cancer each year are caused by exposure to residual pesticides in food. Those same pesticides can be present in the groundwater used for drinking water.

FOCUS What effect would restricting pesticide use have on agriculture and on the economy?

5-4 The corn worm is an example of a pest that attacks crops.

THE CALIFORNIA STORY

One area where groundwater is contaminated with pesticides is California's San Gabriel Valley, located about 20 kilometers east of Los Angeles. At the 1989 Congressional hearing on groundwater contamination, Representative Esteban Torres of California described the San Gabriel region as having some of the worst groundwater contamination in the United States.

If people had known pesticides wouldn't break down over time, California's problem with pesticides would have been predictable. While California takes almost half of its drinking water from groundwater, agriculture uses 5 times that amount of groundwater for irrigation. At the same time, California agriculture uses 50 percent of the pesticides used in the whole United States each year. Because the soil is sandy and porous, the irrigation water carries the pesticides into California's groundwater.

The water district for the San Gabriel Valley area is called the Main San Gabriel Groundwater Basin. Timothy Jochem, project manager at the Main San Gabriel Groundwater Basin, attributed the groundwater contamination not only to past agricultural activities, but also to such things as industrial discharges, leaking chemical storage facilities, illegal dumping, and poorly-designed landfills.

The EPA estimates that cleaning up the Basin's water could cost $800 million and take decades to accomplish.

California's groundwater problem is not confined to the San Gabriel Valley. California's Department of Pesticide Regulation maintains a statewide database of water wells that have been sampled for pesticide contamination. In 1991, 1556 wells in 30 counties were analyzed. The samples showed the presence of 20 pesticides in the groundwater of many of the wells.

On the other hand, California produces more farm income than any other state. Its total earnings from crops is almost double the earnings from the next most productive state. Much of the country's produce is grown in the fertile valley fields, which are sprayed with pesticides and treated with fertilizers. Those chemicals can be the difference between productive fields and ones devastated by pests or poor crop yield.

A Problem with Paint

Pesticides aren't the only problem pollutant. In May 1987, a fire broke out in a Dayton, Ohio, paint warehouse. In the first few hours, public attention was focused on the fire fighters battling to quickly and safely put out the raging fire. However, Dayton residents soon learned that the fire was an even greater disaster than they had first thought. The fire had contaminated their water supply.

Some groundwater supplies are extremely vulnerable to contamination. The warehouse in Dayton had been built in an industrial park on vacant land surrounding Dayton's field of water wells. The same geologic factors that made it cost-effective to put the water wells in this location also made this an area where groundwater could be contaminated very easily. The aquifer was just 3 meters below the ground in some places — easily reached by the hazardous materials in the water spilling out of the gutted warehouse.

The contamination of Dayton's aquifer from the warehouse fire was quickly contained. But as city officials began looking more closely at their water supply, it became clear that the problem was more widespread than they had thought. The fire was not the only source of pollutants. For many years, abandoned sand and gravel quarries at other locations had been used as dump sites for hazardous materials. As these materials leaked into the aquifer below, they entered the drinking water supply of almost one million people.

Dayton reacted to this threat by instituting zoning laws restricting certain types of land use in areas where groundwater was vulnerable to contamination. Properties were "rated" based on how easily groundwater could be polluted at that location. Some locations were permitted for use of hazardous materials. However, locations above the aquifer were protected from potentially dangerous uses such as paint warehouses, dry cleaners, and auto shops.

CONNECTIONS
HEALTH

The California Public Interest Research Group (CALPIRG) has suggested that California's Department of Health Services should be authorized to enforce groundwater regulations rather than the Department of Food and Agriculture. Why would CALPIRG prefer a health services department to oversee groundwater quality rather than leaving it in the hands of the state's agriculture department?

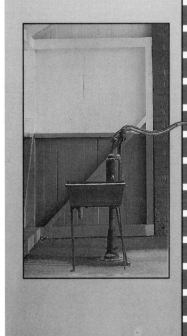

Reactions from Dayton's business community were mixed. The restrictions were backed by the Dayton Area Chamber of Commerce. However, some businesses resented having to take their plans for plant expansions before the new board of environmental managers. Others complained that the rules made it more difficult for them to do business in the city. One disgruntled businessman said, "What they want for Harrison Township is grassland over the [entire] aquifer." ◄

DRINKING FROM THE GLASS

There are many water-use strategies that may be used to protect groundwater before it becomes polluted. Dayton's zoning restrictions are just one example. Farmers can grow more pest-resistant crops, reducing their need for pesticides. In the garden, natural pest controls — such as ladybugs — can replace pesticide sprays.

> **FOCUS** ▶
> Do you think other cities might try to capitalize on this sentiment and lure the businesses who are avoiding cities with environmental zoning such as Dayton's?

A contaminated groundwater supply is very difficult and expensive to return to usable condition. Groundwater does not clean itself quickly, and its location underground makes it difficult for people to aid in that cleansing process. For smaller areas, groundwater can be cleaned by injecting bacteria to break down organic pollutants. Sometimes groundwater can be repeatedly pumped out, cleaned, and then reinjected until the pollutants are flushed out of the aquifer. This can be expensive. The clean-up following the Dayton fire was estimated to cost the paint company over $10 million. Cleaning up after that same fire in a building located on top of a non-porous bed of clay might have cost only $10 000 to $15 000.

Is an area with environmental restrictions designed to protect the health of citizens a healthy environment for business? There are signs that businesses may choose other cities over Dayton when looking for a site on which to build a plant. Their reason would be to avoid what they see as the potential interference of additional environmental laws and restrictions.

Perhaps one way to think of groundwater use is to imagine withdrawing money that has been slowly and steadily accumulating in a savings account over many years. In the short-term, the money is useful. However, it could take many years to replace those savings. Perhaps the savings can never be replaced. The groundwater your city uses today may have been accumulating in its aquifer for centuries. It can be used up — or polluted to the point that it can never be used again — in a much shorter time.

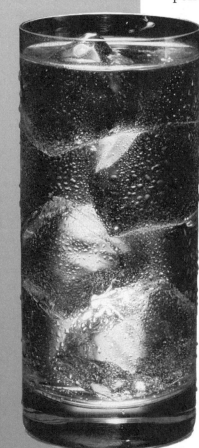

ANALYSIS

IDENTIFY THE PROBLEM
- List and describe the long-term and short-term costs and benefits of using pesticides. What are the costs and benefits of Dayton's zoning restrictions?
- Compare and contrast the groundwater pollution problems experienced by Dayton, Ohio, and by the state of California. How are the pollution causes similar?
- Why couldn't Dayton's solution to its groundwater pollution be applied to the San Gabriel Valley?

LOOKING MORE CLOSELY: ISSUES
- Should pesticides be banned? What would happen if farmers were no longer able to use pesticides? Should pesticide use be limited while alternatives are being developed? How does the world's rapidly-growing population influence your answer?
- Does a farmer own all the water under his or her land? How does the ability of groundwater to move through an aquifer affect the idea of ownership based on surface boundaries?

IN GREATER DEPTH: SCIENCE
- Research the new pesticide alternatives, including such things as insect sterilization. What are the advantages and drawbacks to each method of protecting produce from pests?

PLOTTING THE FUTURE
- Using the data in the table on page 83 of the *Almanac*, graph the change in United States population between 1950 and 1990.
- Using the data in the table on page 84 of the *Almanac*, graph the amount of groundwater used in the United States between 1965 and 1985. Surface water use was down in 1985 due to a drought. Should this have increased or decreased groundwater use for that year? Explain your answer.

ACTING ON THE ISSUES

GROUNDWATER AND YOUR COMMUNITY
- How deep is the water table in your area? Is it rising or falling?
- Is the groundwater in your community used for drinking water?
- Is your community's groundwater contaminated? If it is, what was the source of the contamination?
- What measures can your community adopt to prevent additional or future contamination of the groundwater?

No Room in the Bin

by Burkhard Bilger

GETTING STARTED

- What are the sources of solid waste? What becomes of the solid waste you throw away?
- Why is there a worldwide landfill crisis?
- What are the advantages and disadvantages of disposable products?

Back in 1987, the fate of a barge called *Mobro 4000* was the focus of many people's attention. Every time the television news came on, the *Mobro* seemed to be floating into yet another port. From New York the barge was towed south to North Carolina — then on to Florida, Alabama, Mississippi, and finally around the Gulf of Mexico to Central America. But no port was willing to take on the *Mobro's* cargo— over 3000 tons of garbage. It had been more garbage than the landfill in the Long Island town of Islip could handle. Now it was a problem on the move — a problem *no one* wanted to accept.

At first, the *Mobro's* predicament was an international joke. To some, when the *Mobro* tried to unload its cargo in Mexico and then Belize, it seemed to symbolize the willingness of the United States to sweep its problems under the rug of poor, neighboring countries. To others, it was more simply a symbol of a very real problem: the United States was running out of space for its solid waste.

Six months after it left New York, the *Mobro* was finally ordered back home. The decision had been made to incinerate the garbage in Brooklyn and bury the ash on Long Island. As the barge chugged along New York's shores, members of Greenpeace, an environmental group, hung a banner across the *Mobro's* bow that read: "Next Time...Try Recycling." Can all solid waste be recycled? If not, what should become of it?

This case study will show you how one of the world's most familiar businesses — McDonald's — has tried to cut down on waste without sacrificing customer convenience. You will read how environmental studies and consumer pressure influenced McDonald's to change how it packaged food — not once, but twice. In what ways is pollution created as products journey from factory to user to landfill?

Publication excerpts used by permission of McDonald's Corporation and the Environmental Defense Fund.

CASE STUDY

BOXES FOR BURGERS

Fastfood has become a symbol of the modern, industrialized lifestyle. Perhaps the most famous and best known symbol of fastfood is McDonald's restaurant. In 1955, Dick and Mac MacDonald

6-1 What becomes of the trash you throw away at home, at school, or on the street? The garbage barge, *Mobro 4000*, was a harsh reminder of how difficult it is becoming to dispose of the world's solid waste.

created a restaurant with a cheap, 15-item menu. Service was designed to be fast and the food was packaged to be taken away from the restaurant to be eaten. The ceramic plates, cloth napkins, and metal cutlery used in restaurants in the 1950s had been replaced by disposable wrappers, paper bags, paper napkins, and plastic utensils.

McDonald's catered to a society obsessed with cars, commuting, and instant cooking. The restaurant became a phenomenon. Under new ownership, the McDonald's chain grew rapidly in the decades that followed. More than 13 000 McDonald's restaurants were built worldwide, serving more than 90 billion customers.

However, the very innovations that created the McDonald's empire soon threatened to undermine it. During the 1970s, the growing environmental movement was taking aim at what it called the "throwaway life-style." McDonald's — a major producer of solid waste — became one of this movement's main targets.

THE CURSE OF CONVENIENCE

Think about the amount of solid waste you produce each day. It's easy to recognize the paper you throw away in class as solid waste. Maybe you also remember to include that apple core that was left from your lunch. But your daily total of solid waste also includes things you might not think of as easily. The boxes used to transport apples from the orchards to the grocery may end up as solid waste in a landfill. Even the clothes you wear involved packaging — the boxes used to ship the clothes from the manufacturer to the store, and the bag you used to carry the clothes home — that might become waste. ◀

The amount of solid waste produced in the United States each year is staggering. The average family's junk mail alone consumes one and one-half trees every year. All together more than 350 million kilograms of residential trash are produced every day in the United States alone!

The United States is the world's second-largest exporter of merchandise. Waste is also produced as a by-product of production. It follows that the United States ranks as one of the world's highest waste producers. However, the amount of waste that actually gets buried in landfills is not necessarily set in stone. Today some developed societies recycle more of their waste than others, leading to less actual wasted materials. For instance, the average American produces about 1.5 kilograms of garbage every day and recycles only 10 percent of it. By comparison, the average Japanese citizen produces about 1.0 kilograms of trash each day and recycles 50 percent

---

Is the production of solid waste avoidable? What are the trade-offs involved in balancing an industrial economy with waste reduction?

FOCUS ▶

CULTURAL CONNECTION

of it. As an island nation — even an industrialized nation — Japan has little land to spare for landfills.

THE SWITCH TO FOAM

In the late 1970s, McDonald's commissioned studies and sought advice about their solid waste from scientists and environmentalists. ▶ What McDonald's found in these studies twice changed the way it packaged its products and dealt with wastes.

In 1976, McDonald's commissioned an independent consultant, the Stanford Research Institute, to study environmental measures that McDonald's restaurants could take. The study convinced McDonald's to switch from cardboard to polystyrene foam packaging. Until 1990, the company distributed brochures entitled *McDonald's Packaging: The Facts* that summarized some of the reasons for the switch.

> ...SOME IMPORTANT FACTS ABOUT POLYSTYRENE FOAM PACKAGING THAT WE'VE LEARNED...
>
> 1. *All polystyrene foam and paper packaging used by all quick-service restaurants equals only one-quarter of one percent of what's in a sanitary landfill.*
>
> That's what was revealed by archeological "digs" of several existing landfills by anthropology professor Dr. William Rathje of the University of Arizona. Dr. Rathje has excavated a number of modern landfills throughout the country to determine what actually occurs in a landfill — especially with regard to the biodegradation process — and what materials comprise a landfill. As Dr. Rathje said in a *Washington Times* article, "A lot of bans have been proposed for styrofoam, but it only takes up one-quarter of 1 percent of landfill volume, which is not a lot." ...While foam appears to be bulky, it is 90% air, and compresses easily under the weight of a landfill...

Why does the McDonald's brochure start off discussing the amount of landfill space taken up by polystyrene foam? As of 1992, 76 percent of all solid waste in the United States is put into landfills. Landfills are areas of land where solid waste is dumped, compacted by heavy machinery, and covered

FOCUS

What would motivate a company to take such actions?

CONNECTIONS
EARTH SCIENCE

For information on sanitary landfills, see the *Almanac* entry on page 85.

6-2 Polystyrene food containers keep food warm. However, polystyrene does not decay rapidly, especially in landfills.

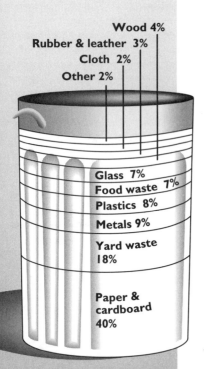

6-3 Relative amounts of solid waste in landfills by weight (EPA, 1988)

CONNECTIONS
CHEMISTRY

Polystyrene is a hard plastic polymer that is easily molded and is a good insulator of heat. This makes it ideal for use in food containers. Polystyrene is an organic compound. For more information on organic compounds, see the *Almanac* entry on page 81.

with earth. There is a worldwide landfill crisis, and it has less to do with mass than with volume. Even with the garbage being compacted, a landfill will hold only so much garbage before it must be closed. Landfills are closing at a dramatic rate. While a small number of new landfills open each year, many more are closed forever. By 1995, it is estimated that 75 percent of the country's landfills will be full.

Therefore, when the McDonald's brochure says that polystyrene foam takes up very little space in a landfill — or that it compacts to fill an even smaller volume — it is saying that the foam products are not contributing in a major way to the landfill crisis.

> **2.** *Polystyrene plastic foam is 100% recyclable.*
> Polystyrene foam is easily recycled. Recycled polystyrene is made into a wide range of useful products like serving trays, insulation board, carpet fibers, video cassettes, hangers, letter trays, and waste receptacles. It also can be combined with other recycled plastics to make a versatile plastic lumber. Polystyrene is being effectively recycled in various areas throughout the United States and overseas...
>
> **3.** *Substitutes for foam packaging are not easily recyclable.*
> The principal substitute for foam packaging would be paper or paperboard products coated with plastic, wax, or other barriers. These materials are not recyclable, as they have to be re-separated into paper and plastic, a process which is not presently commercially feasible. Experts stress the use of a single, non-laminated or coated packaging material (glass, aluminum, polystyrene or paper) to facilitate recycling.

The way to prolong the life of a landfill is to decrease the amount of solid waste put into it. A company may decide to use less packaging for its product. Another way to reduce waste is to recycle more of the waste that gets produced or to increase the amount that gets burned in incinerators.

When it decided to switch to polystyrene foam packaging, McDonald's also began a pilot recycling program. Collection bins were placed near the exits so that the waste could be separated into paper, plastic, and polystyrene foam. Every piece of polystyrene that McDonald's recycled was one less piece that went into one of the nations's overtaxed landfills.

> **4.** *McDonald's polystyrene foam packaging does not contain nor is it manufactured with fully halogenated chlorofluorocarbons (CFCs).*

> McDonald's was the first foodservice organization to voluntarily phase out the use of fully halogenated CFCs, beginning in 1987. (CFCs are chlorofluorocarbons which reduce the Earth's upper ozone layer...)

Before the mid-1980s, plastic foam products were "puffed up" using CFCs, which are thought to break down in Earth's atmosphere, leading to the eventual and gradual destruction of the ozone layer. By using foam packaging that did not contain CFCs, McDonald's eliminated one more argument against using the foam.

> **5.** *Plastic packaging has important health and safety advantages.*
> The Food and Drug Administration (FDA) establishes rigid requirements for materials that are used in food handling. Foam is particularly well-suited for food service because it is manufactured under highly sanitary conditions, and is non-absorbent and will not support bacteria.
>
> Plastic packaging is not subject to the sanitary uncertainties of dishwashing and handling, and does not crack or break in normal usage... ▶
>
> **6.** *What About Biodegradability?*
> Biodegradable plastic packaging is suggested by some to be an appropriate substitute. However, such packaging has not yet met FDA standards for food packaging...
>
> Biodegradation in landfills is an extremely slow process and does not create additional landfill space. Landfills are not compost piles where exposure to air, water, and microorganisms can cause a product to break down. Modern landfills are packed densely and covered with layers of compacted dirt; little water and air can penetrate them.... Scientific digs into landfills in California, Arizona, and Illinois retrieved newspapers which were completely readable after 20 years, corn cobs with kernels intact, and currency usable after more than 10 years....

McDonald's chose to use polystyrene foam over either plastic or paper-based packaging. McDonald's chose not to use biodegradable plastics. One problem is that biodegradable plastics break apart only under particular conditions. A piece of plastic discarded by the side of the road — exposed to light, air, and water — is in the ideal location for biodegradation. However, that same piece of plastic buried in a sanitary landfill — away from light, air, and water — may take hundreds of years to break apart. Biodegradable plastics are also not as strong as other plastics, requiring the use of more plastic to make the same product.

CONNECTIONS
CHEMISTRY
For information on CFCs, see the *Almanac* entry on page 77. For more information on ozone destruction, be sure to read Case Study 1.

FOCUS
Why is it important to use packaging that doesn't crack? Should you serve food in cracked mugs or on cracked plates? Why not?

CONNECTIONS
PHYSICS

A BTU is a British Thermal Unit. A BTU is the amount of heat required to raise the temperature of one pound of water one degree Fahrenheit. Even though it is not a metric unit of measurement, many quantities related to energy — for example, energy consumption and the amount of energy produced by different fuels — are still measured in BTUs.

7. *Polystyrene foam is generally environmentally superior to manufacture than paper.*

Paper mills consume more energy and produce much more wastewater than do polystyrene foam manufacturing plants. They also require harvesting trees for pulp.

A study conducted by Franklin and Associates, a consultant to the United States Environmental Protection Agency, revealed that if the plastic products they studied were replaced with non-plastic alternative products, total energy consumption would [increase] by 834.2 trillion BTU, enough energy to heat nearly four million homes — equal to the number of homes in the greater New York City area — for one year.

9. *Regardless of where people eat and how the food is packaged, the environment is affected.*

Every source of food and meals has some environmental impact.... Even a meal prepared at home requires energy and packaging, and creates waste. Using disposable items obviously results in a effective means of water conservation, since restaurant dishwashers consume very large amounts of water....

9. *Polystyrene foam packaging is safer and less expensive to incinerate than paper.*

In a modern incinerator that is properly maintained and operated, polystyrene foam produces harmless, non-toxic ash (it's mostly air to begin with), carbon dioxide, and water vapor. Because it burns so efficiently, it even acts as a secondary fuel source, making the incinerator hotter and less expensive to run and actually creates a cleaner burning process....

Solid waste can be a source of energy when burned in incinerators. Denmark, for example, burns about half of its solid waste in incinerators designed to change the thermal energy into electricity. Nearly 80 percent of the incinerators in the United States are some type of "waste-to-energy" incinerator. That percentage is growing as older incinerators that did not harness the energy of burning trash are shut down or refurbished.

Incineration has other advantages. Burning does not completely destroy solid waste. However, it does reduce the volume of the waste by an average of 70 percent. The ash that remains takes up less space in the landfill. Burning solid waste also kills germs.

Still, people are not rushing to build incinerators outside of every town and city in the United States. Modern, state-of-the-art incinerators are expensive to build. They must be equipped with complex air pollution controls to remove the pollutants that might

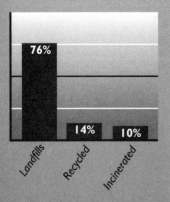

6-4 Most solid waste in the United States eventually goes into landfills.

otherwise be released through their smokestacks. These pollutants include toxic metals — such as lead, mercury, and cadmium — as well as known cancer-causing compounds such as dioxins. These substances are also present in the ash, that gets buried in landfills. Since the burning process actually concentrates the toxic materials in the ash, many people feel that incinerator ash should be buried in landfills specially designed for hazardous waste, not in ordinary landfills.

PAPER CHASE

In the late 1980s, public opinion turned against polystyrene foam and incineration. Working with an environmental research group called the Environmental Defense Fund (EDF), McDonald's decided to change its hamburger packaging once again — from polystyrene boxes (sometimes called "clamshells") to plastic-coated paper wrappers. In a fact sheet entitled *Why McDonald's Did the Right Thing in Saying No to Foam,* EDF justified McDonald's decision with the following arguments:

- The new paper-based wraps provide a whopping 70 percent or greater reduction in packaging waste relative to foam clamshells. More than 80 percent reduction in secondary packaging (corrugated boxes and other materials used to ship the containers) is also achieved....▶
- The new wrap requires much less energy to produce and creates far fewer air pollutants, water pollutants, and solid waste than the polystyrene foam it is replacing....
- As a laminated material, the wraps are currently non-recyclable. However, it is difficult to

CONNECTIONS
EARTH SCIENCE

For more information on incineration, be sure to read the related case study on the incineration of hazardous wastes, Case Study 7.

The boxes and wrappers used in the restaurant are themselves shipped in boxes. Why would the paper-based wraps require less of this "secondary packaging?"

6-5 More than likely, the trash you throw away is eventually taken to a landfill.

> recycle any food-contaminated material regardless of the material used....
> - Polystyrene is manufactured from benzene and styrene — both very toxic chemicals. Health and environmental impacts can arise from the production, storage, and transport of these chemicals. Benzene causes leukemia; styrene is a neurotoxin and a suspected human carcinogen.
> - By volume, discarded food service polystyrene represents at least one percent of all municipal solid waste — a significant portion for any single category.
> - Recycled plastics are bought and sold on the basis of their weight. Polystyrene's low density makes collection enormously expensive.
> - Food, paper, other plastics, and other contaminants have plagued polystyrene recycling plants, as it is both labor-intensive and requires extensive use of water to separate and wash the incoming material. Even after cleaning, residual food contamination (e.g., grease) poses problems and affects the quality of the final recycled material...

McDonald's decision to switch back to paper created a stir when it was announced in November 1990. Some people called it a victory for the environment. Others said that McDonald's was simply appeasing public opinion by opting for paper.

THE PROOF IS IN THE PACKAGING

Public opinion about foam and paper wasn't the only source of controversy. Scientists seemed to be taking both sides of this argument. Studies comparing polystyrene foam packages to cardboard packages were used to show that foam was really better for the environment. The EDF countered that while foam cups might be less polluting than paper cups, paper wrappers were still less polluting than foam "clamshell" packages.

More than anything else, the controversy showed that there are no simple solutions to packaging problems. A company such as McDonald's might not necessarily be able to make one decision about packaging that is the best decision for every location. For example, polystyrene foam may be best for a city that is very close to a polystyrene recycling plant. How and where a package is thrown away adds another layer of complexity to the decision-making process.

The McDonald's experience with its packaging is a good example of good intentions in conflict with tough choices. It has made everyone take a harder look at the costs of solid waste and the benefits of reducing it. "Here today" is not "gone tomorrow" after all.

CONNECTIONS
EARTH SCIENCE

To help conserve Earth's mineral resources, solid waste can be "mined" to remove usable metals. In high-technology resource recovery plants solid waste is processed to recover iron, aluminum, and other valuable materials. These plants are expensive to build and maintain.

ANALYSIS

IDENTIFY THE PROBLEM
- List the costs and benefits of the different packaging materials discussed in this case.
- Discuss the following: "The landfill crisis is a crisis of volume more than mass."
- On what points do the earlier McDonald's brochure and the EDF fact sheet agree? On what points do they contradict each other? Do the contradictions seem to be based on differing data or on different interpretations of the same data?

LOOKING MORE CLOSELY: ISSUES
- You have been given the job of deciding which type of packaging to use for your fast-food restaurant's hamburger packages. Discuss how those packages' final destinations — whether they are buried in a landfill, burned in an incinerator, or tossed along the roadside as litter — might influence your choice of the best type of packaging material to use. Will every package be disposed of in the same way?

LOOKING MORE CLOSELY: SCIENCE
- Research and describe how biodegradation works. What types of materials naturally biodegrade? What conditions does biodegradation require? How are biodegradable plastics made?

ACTING ON THE ISSUES

GARBAGE IN YOUR OWN BACKYARD?
- Estimate how many kilograms of garbage your family produces each week. How much of that solid waste do you recycle?
- List ways in which you can reduce the amount of solid waste that needs to be disposed of from your home and from your school.
- Research what happens to solid waste in your community. Is the waste incinerated or is it buried in a landfill? If the waste goes to a landfill, how much room is left there and where will the next landfill be located? If the waste is burned, what kind of air pollution controls does the incinerator have? Where is the incinerator ash buried?

Rain Forests Under Siege

by Gloria J. Dyer

GETTING STARTED

- Of what benefit are tropical rain forests to the countries in which they are located? How is this different from the potential benefits to Earth in preserving rain forests?
- What are the biological and social consequences of tropical rain forest destruction?

CONNECTIONS
ECONOMICS

Earth's *developing countries* are those nations which are generally poorer, have economies based on agriculture, and are only beginning to acquire industry and advanced technology.

The Ecuadoran rain forest is unbelievably humid and green. Located in the tropics near Earth's equator, the rain forest is warm year-round. The sunlight is strong, and rainfall is abundant— at least 200 centimeters of rain per year. Brightly-colored birds nest in the trees and monkeys feed on the abundant fruits and insects. Snakes, frogs, lizards, and insects live in the trees and on the ground below. On both a large scale and a small scale, the rain forest is a complex, vital web of life.

You may not live in a rain forest, but you *are* part of the complex interactions of Earth's physical and biological systems. You are also connected to faraway people and places in another way. You live in what is sometimes called a "global economy." One country's exports are another country's imports. For instance, the gasoline in the family car may come from oil reserves beneath Ecuador's tropical rain forest. The wood in your bookshelves may be harvested from rain forests in Malaysia. Such products make up the international trade of developing countries.

The United States has always used its abundant natural resources to maintain or expand its own economy. Other countries are now choosing to use their tropical rain forest resources to maintain or expand their economies. Tremendous forest areas have been cut down and developed to produce revenue.

But can land cleared of its rain forest ever recover and support the same ecosystems? Is that important? In this case study, you will look at the complex problems involved in the use of tropical rain forests as a renewable natural resource. Are the rain forests just a usable natural resource or the threatened foundation of the global environment?

CASE STUDY

UNDER THE CANOPY

Only 60 years ago, there were over 15 million square kilometers of tropical rain forest on Earth. Rain forests covered much of South America, Africa, and southeast Asia. Today only 50 percent of these forests survive. Even that number isn't stable. Currently an area of rain forest the size of Florida is destroyed each year. At the present

7-1 Containing over half of Earth's species, the tropical rain forests are threatened by development and deforestation. What effect does the loss of these forests have on Earth's complex web of life and natural processes?

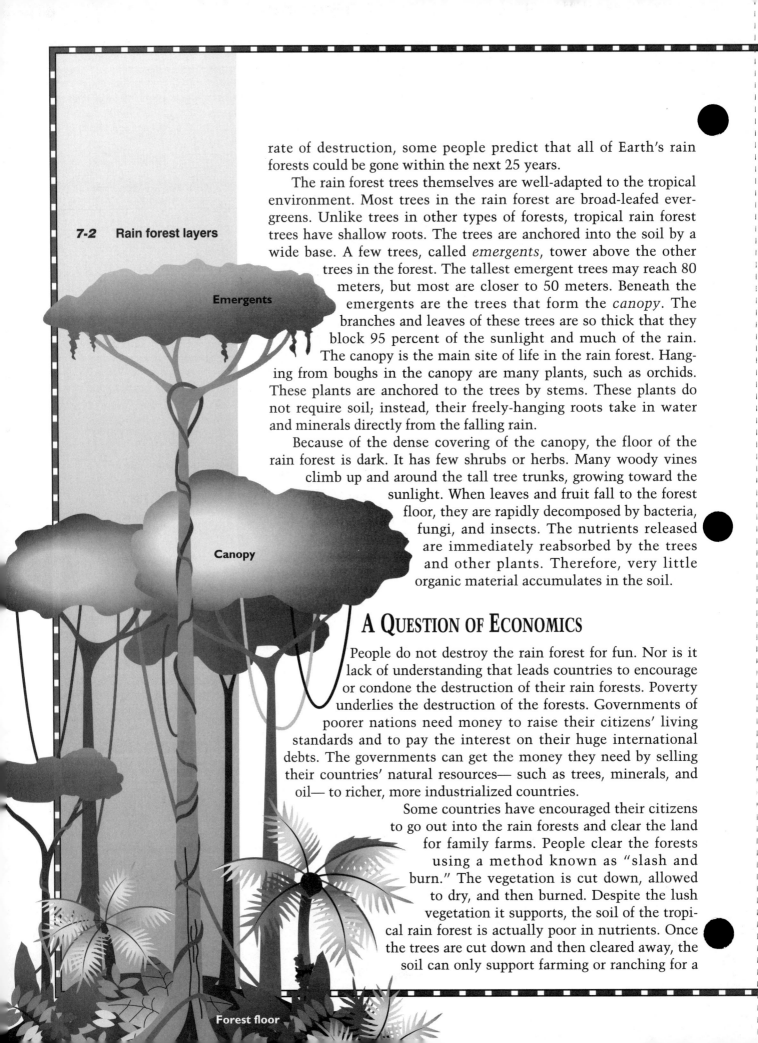

7-2 Rain forest layers

rate of destruction, some people predict that all of Earth's rain forests could be gone within the next 25 years.

The rain forest trees themselves are well-adapted to the tropical environment. Most trees in the rain forest are broad-leafed evergreens. Unlike trees in other types of forests, tropical rain forest trees have shallow roots. The trees are anchored into the soil by a wide base. A few trees, called *emergents*, tower above the other trees in the forest. The tallest emergent trees may reach 80 meters, but most are closer to 50 meters. Beneath the emergents are the trees that form the *canopy*. The branches and leaves of these trees are so thick that they block 95 percent of the sunlight and much of the rain. The canopy is the main site of life in the rain forest. Hanging from boughs in the canopy are many plants, such as orchids. These plants are anchored to the trees by stems. These plants do not require soil; instead, their freely-hanging roots take in water and minerals directly from the falling rain.

Because of the dense covering of the canopy, the floor of the rain forest is dark. It has few shrubs or herbs. Many woody vines climb up and around the tall tree trunks, growing toward the sunlight. When leaves and fruit fall to the forest floor, they are rapidly decomposed by bacteria, fungi, and insects. The nutrients released are immediately reabsorbed by the trees and other plants. Therefore, very little organic material accumulates in the soil.

A Question of Economics

People do not destroy the rain forest for fun. Nor is it lack of understanding that leads countries to encourage or condone the destruction of their rain forests. Poverty underlies the destruction of the forests. Governments of poorer nations need money to raise their citizens' living standards and to pay the interest on their huge international debts. The governments can get the money they need by selling their countries' natural resources— such as trees, minerals, and oil— to richer, more industrialized countries.

Some countries have encouraged their citizens to go out into the rain forests and clear the land for family farms. People clear the forests using a method known as "slash and burn." The vegetation is cut down, allowed to dry, and then burned. Despite the lush vegetation it supports, the soil of the tropical rain forest is actually poor in nutrients. Once the trees are cut down and then cleared away, the soil can only support farming or ranching for a

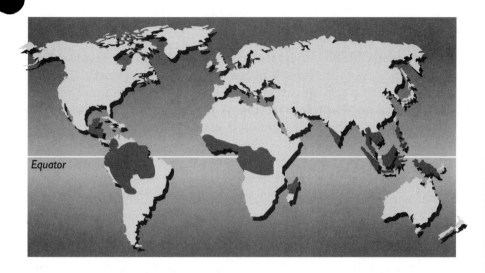

7-3 Tropical rain forests (shaded areas) are found on seven percent of Earth's surface.

few years. To survive, the farmers expand farther into the rain forest. They chop down trees for the wood they need for fuel and for building. As the soil loses its ability to grow crops or support livestock, the farmers must move on to "slash and burn" new areas of the rain forest.

New industries, brought in to provide jobs for the people, can also contribute to deforestation. For example, wood is used in mining and brick making. Smelting iron requires charcoal, which is made from wood. Hydroelectric dam projects destroy tropical rain forests by flooding the river valleys.

BIODIVERSITY AND DEFORESTATION

The greatest environmental concern with rain forest destruction is the loss of biodiversity. *Biodiversity* refers to the variety of organisms living in an ecosystem. An easier way of thinking about biodiversity is to use the number of species in a community and their relative abundance. The actual number of species on Earth is unknown. However, estimates range from 5 million to 50 million. Of that number, only 1.5 million species have been identified. Scientists estimate that two thirds of Earth's plant and animal species may make their home in tropical rain forests. Small populations of individual species are vulnerable to extinction with only the slightest change in their habitats. With the loss of these important rain forest ecosystems, thousands— perhaps millions— of species will become extinct before they are identified.

Other problems occur after deforestation. Without the lush rain forest vegetation to help the ground absorb the water, flooding may occur. Bangladesh is a low-lying country, etched by the distributaries of the Ganges and Brahmaputra River deltas. Deforestation of the watersheds in Bangladesh has worsened the already severe flooding. A flood in 1975 killed an estimated half million people.

CONNECTIONS
METEOROLOGY

Computer models of the Amazon rain forest suggest that once the forest is destroyed it will probably never recover. The models show that when the forest is cleared for pasture land, surface temperatures increase. Precipitation decreases. These local climate changes make it difficult to regrow a tropical forest.

CONNECTIONS
BIOLOGY

For more information on ecosystems and habitats, see the *Almanac* entry on page 86. For more information on extinction, see the *Almanac* entry on page 86.

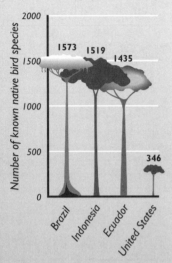

7-4 Countries with rain forests have greater biodiversity.

In a loan of money, what is the difference between *principal* and *interest*? If you only pay interest, does the debt ever go away?

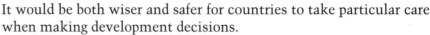

It would be both wiser and safer for countries to take particular care when making development decisions.

Deforestation also increases the loss of topsoil by erosion. Erosion washes away the topsoil necessary for forest regrowth. The soil is washed into rivers and streams where it chokes channels and disrupts the rivers' own ecosystems. A change in one ecosystem can affect another, apparently unrelated, ecosystem.

ECUADOR'S OIL DILEMMA

Other countries might envy the decisions that Ecuador has had to make. Like other countries, Ecuador is a country with a staggering international debt. However, unlike other countries, Ecuador has large deposits of oil and natural gas. Unfortunately these valuable resources are located under the tropical rain forests in the eastern part of the country.

The discovery of oil was a windfall for the Ecuadoran economy. The petroleum resources were first developed by United States corporations who built a pipeline to transport the petroleum from the inland to the coast for shipment. Ecuador began to export petroleum during the 1970s. Half of the oil produced in Ecuador in the 1980s was exported to the United States. Today petroleum makes up 35 percent to 65 percent of Ecuador's total exports.

Presently the large amount of money Ecuador receives from oil exports does little or nothing to reduce the country's international debt. In the 1980s, Ecuador's debt increased due to inflation, a global slump in the oil industry, and a series of devastating earthquakes. Now, like so many countries, Ecuador is struggling to keep up with just the interest payments on the money it owes. ◀

The oil exploration in Ecuador sometimes has ecological costs. The Ecuadoran government has already allowed the entire eastern rain forest area to be used by foreign oil companies for oil exploration and drilling. Despite government regulations, the rain forests, their ecosystems, and the native cultures dependent on them are all being threatened within the vast drilling areas. The people and animals who live in the rain forest are affected not only by the clearing of the forests for the oil wells, but also by the clearing of trees to make way for roads, pipelines, stores, and houses for the workers. Wildlife and native inhabitants must deal with oil spills that contaminate waterways.

Currently foreign oil companies are exploring in another seven million acres of Ecuadoran rain forest. Part of this new exploration is taking place in Yasuní National Park. Yasuní National Park is one of the Amazon Basin's largest rain forest preserves. It is also home to a group of about 125 Huaorani Indians. Other exploration is taking place within the Huaorani Indian Reserve itself. The Huaorani are a very traditional tribe that lives in northeastern Ecuador. Before the oil exploration began, the Huaorani had limited contact with western culture. The Sierra Club and others worry that the Huaorani face cultural destruction if their territory is not used with proper care.

A Renewable Resource

Ecuador may have more of a problem with biodiversity than other rain forest countries. Part of Ecuador's rain forests are sandwiched between the Pacific Ocean on the west and the Andes Mountains on the east. A larger area of rain forest that lies east of the Andes is called the Oriente. It is part of the Amazon drainage basin and is thought to have the highest biodiversity of any place on Earth. The populations of individual animal species in the Oriente are also very small. Yasuní National Park contains a lush rain forest. It is thought to be of such value that the United Nations Educational, Scientific, and Cultural Organization has declared it a "world biosphere reserve."

To address both problems at once, a country like Ecuador can decide to make money from the rain forest without destroying it. ▶ Such use of the rain forest is referred to as *sustainable development*. Sustainable development uses the rain forest, but also maintains it for future generations. Ecuador's national oil company, Petroecuador, is researching sustainable development in addition to its oil exploration and development efforts.

Agroforestry attempts to combine farming with forest preservation by scattering pastures or crops among the trees. Where this is not possible, smaller areas of cleared land can be kept productive for longer periods of time by using natural fertilizers and natural pest controls. This practice would keep farmers from clearing land, using up the soil's nutrients, and moving on to "slash and burn" additional parts of the forest.

There are other possibilities for sustainable development of the rain forests. Forest reserves can be created. At the center of the reserve, the rain forest would be strictly preserved. Areas farther from the center would be used to a greater degree. Another suggestion is to use the managed forestry practices common in North America. Trees are taken out a few at a time and new trees are planted. This method maintains the forest and prevents soil erosion.

Listening to the Medicine Man

People native to the rain forests— the indigenous population— know an amazing amount about the real wealth of the rain forest. These tribal peoples believe in *shamanism*— the idea that the human spirit is connected to the natural world. Like the Native American medicine man of North America, the tribal shaman is

7-5 Geographic areas of Ecuador

FOCUS

What are the incentives for a country like Ecuador to preserve the rain forest?

CONNECTIONS
BIOLOGY

A scientist who studies the relationship between plants and people is called an *ethnobotanist*. To conserve the genetic resources of plants for the use of future scientists, researchers are storing plant genes, embryos, and seeds in "banks."

CONNECTIONS
ECONOMICS

Products harvested from rain forests include rubber, vanilla, cocoa, coffee, Brazil nuts, avocados, quinine, and chicle. You know chicle as the substance that makes chewing gum chewable.

both mystical leader and healer for his people, drawing upon centuries-old knowledge of the healing properties of plants.

Using tropical plants and animals for medicine is another example of sustainable use for the rain forests. Medical researchers from around the world are making frequent visits to the rain forest and the native healers who live there. The researchers collect samples of the healing plants recommended by the tribal shamans. Some samples are sent to scientists at the National Cancer Institute who test the plants for use as possible cures for cancer. Over one-third of all anticancer drugs currently in use had their origin in the tropical rain forests.

Other drugs discovered in the rain forest are already in use. Curare is a medicine made from the curare vine. Natives in the Amazon use curare to make a poison for the tips of their arrows. Curare is now being used as a muscle relaxant during surgery. The drug reserpine comes from snakeroot, a plant used by natives to calm anxiety. Reserpine is used as a tranquilizer and a treatment for high blood pressure (hypertension).

There are two ideas for using rain forest medicinal resources. Medicinal plants can be raised by agroforestry methods and harvested for sale to pharmaceutical companies. Another method may be to have the active chemicals identified from plant samples and then produced synthetically by the pharmaceutical companies. Those companies then would pay a percentage of their sales to the country in which the plant was discovered. The income would allow that country's government to repay more of its international debt or to protect vast areas of rain forest.

SEARCHING FOR SOLUTIONS

There is no single solution to managing Earth's tropical rain forests. Each solution will be unique to a given area and economy. But, solutions are available. The desire exists to preserve the rain forest and the culture of the indigenous peoples who live there. Developed countries must help the developing countries find ways to prosper economically so that the developing countries can conserve their natural resources, preserve both natural species and native cultures, and help protect what may be the well-being of Earth's global environment.

ANALYSIS

IDENTIFY THE PROBLEM
- Why do nations allow the clearing of their tropical rain forests? What happens to the money the governments receive from the development of their rain forests?
- What are the arguments against destroying tropical rain forests? What happens to the ecosystems when deforestation occurs? What becomes of the indigenous peoples who live in the forest?
- How would the biodiversity found in a rain forest influence your decision whether or not to clear the forest for farmland?

LOOKING MORE CLOSELY: ISSUES
- Bolivia is participating in a *debt-for-nature* swap in which part of the country's foreign debt is canceled in exchange for an agreement to preserve land. (Another possibility is to pay off part of a debt in exchange for the country granting land rights to the indigenous peoples.) Should developed countries tell less developed countries what to do with their natural resources? If not, what *should* developed countries do?

IN GREATER DEPTH: SCIENCE
- Research the connection between rain forest destruction and global warming. How does rain forest destruction add greenhouse gases to Earth's atmosphere? How do the rain forest plants help remove carbon dioxide from the atmosphere?

PLOTTING THE FUTURE
- Using the rain forest data on page 86 of the *Almanac*, calculate how many years it would take to totally destroy all rain forests in Madagascar, the tropical South American countries, and Central Africa. Assume the annual rate of deforestation will remain the same as it was during the 1980s.

ACTING ON THE ISSUE

THE POLITICS OF BIODIVERSITY
- Research the June, 1992, meeting of the United Nations Conference on Environment and Development in Rio de Janeiro, Brazil. (The conference was known in the popular press as "The Earth Summit.")
- At the Earth Summit, the United States government refused to sign the non-binding declaration on biodiversity. What reasons were given?
- Has the United States' government position on biodiversity changed since 1992? Write to the President or to your members of Congress to voice your support or displeasure with the current position.

Trouble in the Sound

by Robert F. Ehrhardt

GETTING STARTED

- What are the sources of the water pollution problems in Long Island Sound?
- What roles do scientific models play in solving real-world problems?
- Do you need conclusive proof that someone or something is causing water pollution before you can take steps to control it? How would the seriousness of the pollution damage being done affect your answer?

Sailboats skim the sparkling surface of the waves on the far horizon. Portable CD players fill the warm air with the sounds of rock and rap. The smell of food is everywhere — fresh popcorn and hot dogs sizzling on the grill. Kids and parents dodge sand castles and volleyball games on their way to the refreshment stand. It's a perfect day at the beach, except for one thing — nobody is in the water. The water is too polluted.

Every year water pollution closes beaches along lakes, rivers, bays, and oceans. That pollution comes in many forms and from many sources. Factories, refineries, and sewage treatment plants are familiar sources of water pollution. Other sources — such as farms — may not come to mind as easily. Even the lawns in front of suburban homes can pollute the water.

One body of water currently afflicted by a variety of pollutants is Long Island Sound. The Sound is a small piece of the Atlantic Ocean, located between the Connecticut shoreline and Long Island, New York. Millions of people — ten percent of the United States population — live within easy driving distance of the Sound. They look forward to swimming, fishing, or boating in its waters in the summertime. They enjoy the shellfish harvested from the Sound's waters.

But today the Sound's waters are in trouble. Fewer fish are caught now than 20 years ago. More beaches are closed. The water is polluted. In this case study, you will examine how people who depend on Long Island Sound for their jobs and recreation are trying to solve its water pollution problems. As you will see, pinpointing the cause of a problem is not always easy. Choosing the right solution to a problem can be harder still.

CASE STUDY

THE BOUNTIFUL SOUND

Try to imagine a saltwater swimming pool 150 kilometers long and up to 32 kilometers wide. That's almost the size of Delaware! The pool is 30 meters deep at the shallow end and over 90 kilometers at the deep end. This mental picture should give you some idea of the size and volume of Long Island Sound. Located only a commuter

8-1 Beaches, such as this one on New York's Long Island, are enjoyable places to spend the day. However, water pollution has caused many beaches to be closed for days, weeks — sometimes an entire vacation season.

8-2 Location of Long Island Sound.

CONNECTIONS
BIOLOGY
For more information on estuaries, see the *Almanac* entry on page 87.

CONNECTIONS
EARTH SCIENCE
For more information on the water cycle, see the *Almanac* entry on page 87.

train ride away from New York City and a short drive from much of Connecticut, the Sound is close enough for millions of people to use its beaches each year. Others fish in the Sound's waters — some for sport, some to make a living.

Much of Long Island Sound's value lies not in its use to people but rather as a habitat for plants and animals. Long Island Sound is an estuary — a dynamic, tidal ecosystem with salt marshes, mud flats, bays, islands, bluffs, and beaches. Estuaries are home to a wide variety of wildlife. The waters and floor of the Sound support a rich population of blue and red crabs, sand shrimp, clams, oysters, and even lobsters. Blackfish and flounder are among the fish species that use the Sound as a spawning ground in the spring. Bluefish, striped bass, and Atlantic salmon are found in the Sound in great numbers throughout the year.

TROUBLED WATERS

Unfortunately Long Island Sound has another major use — waste disposal. Over forty sewage treatment plants dump their waste water into the Sound. Some of these treatment plants are located along the shores and have discharge pipes that extend out into the water not far from shore. Other sewage waste water reaches the Sound indirectly. The Connecticut, Housatonic, and Thames rivers empty into the Sound, carrying pollutants that were dumped or washed into these rivers tens of kilometers upstream.

Dumping sewage and other pollutants into rivers or into the ocean is not a new practice. In theory, pollutants become diluted in a larger body of water. Two spoonfuls of sugar in a glass of water can taste fairly sweet. But that same amount of sugar dissolved in a reservoir of hundreds of thousands of liters of water might never be noticed. In the case of Long Island Sound, sewage treatment plant operators assumed that the water and waves of the Sound would dilute the pollutants in their waste water and render them harmless. Unfortunately, many pollutants — such as some cancer-causing chemicals — are harmful even in extremely dilute concentrations.

The waters of Long Island Sound contain many kinds of pollutants. Heavy metals and organic chemicals were once a big problem for the Sound. A few decades ago, cities on the shores of the Sound — such as Bridgeport, Connecticut — still had many factories, each dumping chemicals into the water. Industries in other cities upstream from the Sound also added their share of pollutants. But much of that pollution has been stopped over the years. Many of the older factories have closed. Others have cleaned up their waste water with pollution control equipment.

THE NITROGEN FACTOR

By the 1980s, the number one pollution problem for Long Island Sound was nitrogen. It may seem odd to think that nitrogen could be a serious pollution problem. After all, most of the air you breathe — about 78 percent — is nitrogen. Nitrogen is an essential nutrient for all forms of life. Its importance as a fertilizer for crops, forests, and virtually all plant life has been known for centuries.

Yet when large amounts of nitrogen are added to a body of water, a condition known as *hypoxia* can occur. In hypoxia, all the oxygen naturally dissolved in the water is used up. Aquatic plants die and marine animals — fish, crabs, lobsters — either leave the area or suffocate.

CONNECTIONS
CHEMISTRY

The amount of a substance contained in a solution is called the *concentration*. Concentrations of pollutants are most often given in parts per million, or *ppm*. A river whose water contains 1 ppm nitrogen would contain 1 part nitrogen per 1 000 000 parts water.

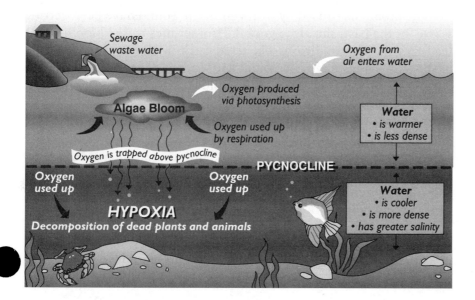

8-3 Hypoxia events are worse in the summer due to warming of the water by the sun, which stengthens the division of the water into two layers with different temperatures and densities. The pycnocline separates these two layers.

How does hypoxia occur? Nitrogen works like a fertilizer in water just as it does on land. Nitrogen stimulates the growth of bacteria, seaweed, algae, and other aquatic plants. Hypoxia begins when the population of oxygen-using bacteria in the water increases due to the addition of nitrogen. These bacteria take so much oxygen from the water that both plants and animals begin to die. As large numbers of plants and animals die and decompose, bacteria break down the organic matter and use even more oxygen from the water. In the end, there is little, if any, oxygen in the water and no marine life left in the area. The decaying animal and plant life in the water and on the shore emit foul-smelling gases, contain bacteria, and attract insects. Swimming in the water or even walking on the beach becomes dangerous to your health.

From up the River

Millions of tons of nitrogen are added to Long Island Sound each year. Where is the nitrogen in Long Island Sound coming from? Scientists think most of that nitrogen comes from sewage treatment plants. Modern sewage treatment removes almost all the harmful or unwanted materials from sewage. However, the waste water from sewage plants still contains nitrogen. By some estimates, Connecticut sewage treatment plants pump over seven tons of nitrogen a day into the Sound.

Another source of nitrogen that has not been estimated so precisely is fertilizer. When rain falls on farms and lawns in Connecticut and on Long Island, fertilizer is washed into streams, streets, and storm sewers. From there, it eventually ends up in the Sound. The growth in new housing developments along the Sound's shoreline in the 1960s and 1970s meant that many more lawns were being fertilized than before.

The problems caused by nitrogen in the Sound have been getting worse. In the past, the algae growths (sometimes called *blooms*) that lead to hypoxia conditions occurred only in the summer. But by 1990, nitrogen levels in the Sound had reached the point where large algae growths were occurring in the middle of winter as well.

Planning for Action

Government agencies have been studying the problems caused by nitrogen in Long Island Sound for years. In 1985, Congress asked the Environmental Protection Agency (EPA) and the states of Connecticut and New York to take part in the Long Island Sound Study. The goals of the study were to identify the Sound's water quality problems, pinpoint their causes, and find solutions.

Scientists have tried to develop computer programs that will be able to describe the effects of pollutants on bodies of water, such as

CONNECTIONS
EARTH SCIENCE

Not all the fertilizer washes into streams with the runoff. Some enters and pollutes the groundwater. For more information on groundwater and groundwater pollution, be sure to read Case Study 5 and the *Almanac* entry on page 84.

8-4 This algae bloom in a Wisconsin lake was caused by nitrogen and phosphate pollution.

8-5 This water quality inspector and lab technician are gathering water samples. The samples will be analyzed to find pH and oxygen levels.

Long Island Sound. In effect, these complex programs serve as models of the real body of water and its many conditions. A *model* is something used to convey information about another object, event, or series of events. A globe, for example, is a common physical model of Earth. A properly designed computer model should help answer many important questions. ▶ What sources of nitrogen cause hypoxia conditions? Where and when will hypoxia occur? If it occurs, what will be the effects on marine life?

In the case of Long Island Sound, the model is a computer program being developed by the National Oceanographic and Atmospheric Administration (NOAA). The NOAA model has not been easy to develop. As you know, there are many sources of nitrogen. In addition, most water bodies are very complex systems. They have currents and temperatures that vary with the season, the weather, and the time of day. At best, these models are only a rough approximation of actual conditions in the real body of water.

Computer models are only as good as the quality of the data they use. Many questions have been raised about the data used so far in the Long Island Sound model. There have been problems with the methods used to collect some of the data. Other data are not even part of the model. For instance, the NOAA model does not include the effects of fertilizer runoff. If the model doesn't include all the nitrogen sources, some people wonder whether they can trust the model's predictions.

TWO SIDES

While the NOAA model is still being developed, the preliminary results were used to begin an interim plan that has stabilized nitro-

> ◀ **FOCUS**
>
> A globe models Earth's shape and shows basic geography. It does not model Earth's mass or inner structure. Do models include everything about what they represent? How does the decision about what to include in a model affect its usefulness after completion?

8-6 One method of treating sewage is to trickle the liquids over a bed of rocks or spray it into large tanks. This adds oxygen, which helps bacteria break down waste.

FOCUS ▶

Rivers flow past many towns on their way to the ocean. How does this complicate decisions as to who is responsible for river pollution?

gen levels. Sewage treatment plants were already required to limit the amount of nitrogen they can discharge to the Sound. The interim plan has frozen the amounts of nitrogen permitted for release at present levels. The plan does not require any plant to reduce the amount of nitrogen it discharges. Nor does it require any controls on fertilizer use.

Terry Backer, the Long Island Soundkeeper, thinks more must be done to limit nitrogen discharges. Of the government's plan he said, "It's just not progressive enough. I think we have enough solid evidence and enough circumstantial evidence out there to do...[more]."

On the other side, people argue that not enough is known to rush into making drastic changes or spending large amounts of money. Adrian P. Freund, chief of Connecticut's Office of Long Island Sound Programs, doesn't think that there is enough scientific evidence yet to justify forcing municipalities to reduce their nitrogen discharges. He said, "While everyone wants to reduce nitrogen as soon as possible, I think it would be very difficult to go ahead and set limits until we have the model in place."

Controlling nitrogen in the Sound will not be cheap. It is estimated that $6 to 8 billion would be needed to completely eliminate the Sound's problems with hypoxia. Most of the towns with sewage treatment plants do not have the money for extra pollution control equipment to control nitrogen. ◀ Connecticut has so far set aside $15 million or nitrogen control improvements at several of the treatment plants in its towns. New York would need many times that amount to reduce nitrogen from its many sewage treatment plants. Neither state has yet addressed how to control the much more difficult fertilizer runoff problem.

HURRY UP AND WAIT

The effects of nitrogen pollution are well known. What is not known with certainty is what it will take to eliminate the problems. Which nitrogen sources need controlling and by how much? The computer model now being developed by NOAA will provide answers that will satisfy some people, but probably not all.

In balancing the environment of Long Island Sound against the economic hardships of paying for pollution controls, how long does one wait? The enormous expense of stopping nitrogen pollution in Long Island Sound makes it important for scientists to provide reliable evidence about exactly what is causing the problems and what actions will solve them. Taxpayers cannot afford to pay for "solutions" that may or may not work. At the same time, how wise is it to wait for all the facts to be in? Can the Sound wait for a 100 percent accurate model?

ANALYSIS

IDENTIFY THE PROBLEM
- List the costs and benefits of fixing Long Island Sound's nitrogen problem.
- What is gained by waiting for the NOAA computer model to become more accurate? What are the risks of waiting?
- Does anyone oppose the control of nitrogen pollution in Long Island Sound? Does anyone dispute that nitrogen pollution is occurring in the Sound? What are the two sides of this case?

LOOKING MORE CLOSELY: ISSUES
- When the government determines that a factory is causing water pollution, the factory is usually fined and forced to either stop polluting or shut down. Discharge from town sewage plants and fertilizer from farms and individual homes cause the pollution in Long Island Sound. Neither the towns nor the homeowners have the money required to fix the problems, and they are not going to "shut down." Discuss how the difference between private business and public utilities or an individual's rights affects the types and timing of solutions available to clean up Long Island Sound.

PLOTTING THE FUTURE
- In 1990, the EPA said that the ten worst states for releasing toxic wastes into surface waters (measured in mass dumped) were Louisiana, Washington, California, Illinois, Ohio, Alaska, Tennessee, Texas, Georgia, and Connecticut. Use the data table on *Almanac* page 87 to calculate the percentage of each state's rivers that the EPA considers "fishable." Do the worst states on each list agree? Why might the lists not agree?

ACTING ON THE ISSUES

WHERE DOES IT GO?
- What are the most significant sources of water pollution in your community? How many are "point" sources — a single source that can be located and controlled — such as sewage treatment plants and factories? How many are "non-point" sources such as runoff from farms, streets, and parking lots?
- Does the sewage treatment plant in your community provide primary or secondary treatment? How recently was your community's treatment plant built or substantially renovated/updated?

Almanac

INDEX OF CONTENT ENTRIES

Acid rain, p. 79
Atmosphere, structure of, p. 78
    troposphere
    stratosphere
    mesosphere
    thermosphere
Chemicals, organic and inorganic, p. 81
Chlorofluorocarbons (CFCs), p. 77
Electromagnetic spectrum, p. 77
    gamma rays
    infrared light
    ultraviolet
    visible light
    X rays
Estuaries, p. 87
Extinction, p. 86
    mass extinction
Food chains, p. 79
    food webs
Groundwater, p. 84
    aquifers
    water table
    zone of aeration
    zone of saturation
Hazardous waste, forms and dangers of, p. 81
Living communities, p. 86
    biome
    biosphere
    ecosystem
    habitat
    niche
Ozone, p. 77
pH scale, p. 82
    acid
    base
Pollution credits, p. 82
Sanitary landfills, p. 85
Superfund, p. 81
Taiga, p. 79
Tundra, p. 79
Water cycle, p. 87

TABLES

Amount of CFC-12 Released, 1932-1988, p. 78
Emissions Estimates for EPA-Monitored Pollutants by Source, 1985-1990, p. 83
Energy Consumption Per Person, 1979-1989, p. 80
Hazardous Waste Sites, Partial National Priority List, 1992, p. 81
Municipal Solid Waste, United States, 1960-1988, p. 85
Nitrogen Emissions, 1970-1989, p. 82
Population Size
    Estimated and Projected, 1950-2025, p. 83
    Percent Share of World Population, 1950-2025, p. 83
Sulfur Emissions, 1970-1989, p. 82
Tropical Deforestation, p. 86
Water Quality in Selected States, p. 87
Water Use in the U.S., 1965-1985, p. 84
World Oil Production, 1950-1990, p. 80
World Net Electricity from Nuclear Power Plants, 1950-1990, p. 80

Case Study 1

OZONE: CRISIS AVERTED?

The Electromagnetic Spectrum

Electromagnetic waves travel through empty space at 300 000 kilometers per second. The total range of electromagnetic waves is called the *electromagnetic (EM) spectrum*. Each different electromagnetic wave is identified by its wavelength.

Electromagnetic waves with the shortest wavelengths and greatest energy are called *gamma rays*. Gamma rays have wavelengths that are 100 million times smaller than a human hair.

X rays are electromagnetic waves that have wavelengths a little longer than those of gamma rays. X rays can penetrate all but the very dense parts of your body.

Ultraviolet (UV) radiation has a wavelength between that of X rays and *visible light*. Visible light contains all the colors of a rainbow. Each color corresponds to a different wavelength of light.

Electromagnetic waves with wavelengths slightly longer than visible light are called *infrared light*. Energy from infrared light waves warms Earth.

Microwaves are electromagnetic waves with wavelengths longer than those of infrared light. *Radio waves* can have wavelengths thousands of meters long.

ELECTROMAGNETIC (EM) SPECTRUM

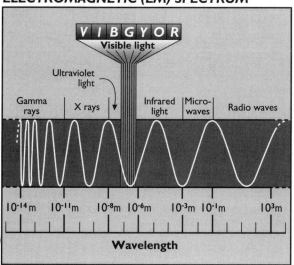

Ozone

UV radiation both creates and destroys ozone. Ozone, O_3, is unstable and decomposes to form O_2 molecules and oxygen atoms in the presence of UV radiation. However, the reaction is reversible. When oxygen molecules absorb energy from either UV radiation or an electric discharge, it forms oxygen atoms. The oxygen atoms can react with oxygen molecules, reforming ozone. As a result, under normal conditions the amounts of ozone remain relatively constant. The decomposition and formation reactions in the stratosphere absorb or filter out much of the sun's UV radiation.

Chlorofluorocarbons (CFCs)

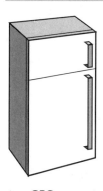

Developed between 1928 and 1930, CFCs were often called wonder chemicals. CFCs were tested and found to be nontoxic, stable, noncorrosive, and nonflammable. CFCs are organic compounds containing hydrogen, carbon, chlorine, and fluorine. To add to their overall appeal, CFCs were inexpensive to produce. As a result of these desirable qualities, CFCs were integral parts of many industries. Until recently, they were used as propellants in aerosol cans. They are still used in refrigeration and in air conditioning. Not until the early 1970s did CFCs begin to lose some of their appeal. Ironically the same qualities that made them industrial wonder chemicals also made them dangerous to Earth's atmosphere.

CFCs are considered the primary suspects in the depletion of ozone. As CFCs migrate to the upper atmosphere, they react with ultraviolet radiation. The chlorine atoms produced then react with ozone. Scientists report that chlorine released into the atmosphere can destroy ozone for decades. A single chlorine atom destroys thousands of ozone molecules.

Amount of CFC-12 Released
(millions of kilograms)

	CFC Source		
Year	Refrigeration	Foam	Aerosols
1932	0.1	0.0	0.0
1934	0.2	0.0	0.0
1936	0.5	0.0	0.1
1938	1.1	0.0	0.1
1940	2.2	0.0	0.1
1942	3.5	0.0	0.2
1944	5.8	0.0	0.4
1946	8.9	0.0	5.1
1948	11.5	0.0	13.2
1950	11.6	0.0	18.0
1952	12.0	0.0	21.6
1954	14.7	0.0	28.1
1956	18.9	0.1	37.2
1958	23.6	0.1	43.2
1960	28.8	0.2	60.0
1962	33.4	0.5	80.7
1964	37.9	1.8	116.3
1966	42.8	2.5	149.7
1968	50.4	3.1	193.1
1970	60.0	4.9	235.5
1972	70.7	6.3	272.9
1974	83.6	9.3	325.8
1976	97.0	8.0	285.3
1978	113.9	14.1	213.4
1980	134.4	21.0	177.1
1982	151.6	22.0	163.6
1984	162.0	28.5	169.0
1986	170.3	34.2	172.0
1988	186.9	59.6	146.2

SOURCE: US DEPARTMENT OF ENERGY, ENVIRONMENTAL SCIENCES DIVISION

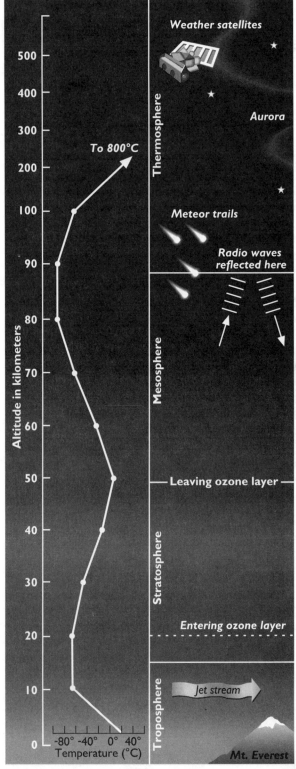

STRUCTURE OF EARTH'S ATMOSPHERE

Structure of the Atmosphere

Scientists divide Earth's atmosphere into four layers based on temperature changes. The lowest layer is called the *troposphere*. The troposphere starts at Earth's surface and its temperature gradually decreases with altitude.

The second layer is the *stratosphere*. The absorption of sunlight by ozone is what makes the stratosphere's temperatures increase with altitude.

The third layer is the *mesosphere*. In the mesosphere, the temperature falls again. The temperature of the atmosphere reaches its lowest point, –90°C.

The fourth layer is the *thermosphere*. Here the temperature rises for the last time. The top is around 500 kilometers from Earth's surface.

Case Study 2

THE JAMES BAY PROJECT

Tundra and Taiga

Just south of the Arctic, in the northern parts of North America, Europe, and Asia, is a treeless region called the *tundra*. Winter on the tundra lasts 6 to 9 months. Temperatures are usually below freezing and the skies are dark. Only during the brief summer does the snow melt. The top meter of tundra soil thaws during the brief summer, but the ground beneath it is permanently frozen. This permanently frozen ground is called *permafrost*. Because of the permafrost, water from melting snow cannot drain into the ground. Instead, it forms many shallow bogs and streams.

Few animals are able to live on the tundra through the harsh winter. Most animals migrate south and return during the summer to breed. Ducks, geese, sandpipers, gulls, and songbirds nest all over the tundra. Herds of caribou and reindeer, musk oxen, and rodents such as lemmings are common.

South of the tundra lies a continuous band of forest made up mostly of conifers. This biome is the *taiga*, or coniferous forest. Like the tundra, the taiga has long, cold winters. Most precipitation is in the form of snow. However, taiga summers are longer and warmer than those in the tundra. The longer summers allow the soil to thaw completely, which allows trees to grow. Like the tundra, the taiga has many bogs and wetlands.

The trees of the taiga provide food and shelter for many animals. Year-round residents include moose, lynx, porcupines, red squirrels, and many small rodents. Many of these animals hibernate during the winter, living off supplies of stored body fat.

Food Chains

Suppose the duckweed in a pond is eaten by a duckling. The duckling is then eaten by a snapping turtle. As one organism eats another, energy is transferred. The transfer of energy from the sun through a series of organisms in an ecosystem is called a *food chain*.

A food chain begins with a producer, such as the duckweed. All succeeding levels in the food chain are made up of consumers. The duckling is a first-order consumer. The snapping turtle is a second-order consumer. The food chain ends when the last consumer dies and is decomposed by microorganisms.

Toxins— either artificial or those found in tiny amounts in nature — grow more concentrated at each level of the food chain. Humans, at the "top" of the food chain, accumulate the highest level of toxins.

Ecosystems contain many food chains. Usually the organisms in one food chain are part of other chains as well. Consider a meadow ecosystem. One food chain may be grass–mouse–snake–hawk. Another food chain in the same meadow may be grass–grasshopper–frog–snake. Several interconnected food chains make up a *food web*.

Acid Rain

Acid rain is caused by pollutants such as sulfur dioxide (SO_2) and nitrogen oxides (NO and NO_2). These gases dissolve in cloud droplets to form sulfuric acid and nitric acid. Acid rain is any form of precipitation that has a pH of less than 5.6.

Acid rain causes far-reaching damage. Over time, acid rain can react with city buildings, slowly eating them away. Acid rain causes soils, streams, and lakes to become more acidic. In the worst cases, acid rain has destroyed forests and makes lakes unlivable for fish.

Sulfur dioxide and nitrogen oxides are given off by cars, power plants, and factories that burn fossil fuels. Reducing the amount of pollutants released by these sources decreases acid rain. The introduction of catalytic converters on automobile exhaust systems has reduced the emissions of nitrogen oxides by 76 percent since 1970. The catalytic converter uses a mixture of platinum-palladium pellets as a catalyst. As nitrogen oxides pass over the pellets, they are changed to nitrogen and oxygen. The pellets serve as catalysts; they are not consumed in the chemical reactions.

For more information on acid rain, see Case Study 4, *Acid on the Wind*.

World Oil Production, 1950–1990

Year	Production (millions of barrels per day)
1950	10.4
1952	12.4
1954	13.7
1956	16.8
1958	18.1
1960	21.0
1962	24.3
1964	28.2
1966	32.9
1968	38.8
1970	45.8
1972	51.0
1974	56.3
1976	58.1
1978	60.7
1980	59.6
1982	53.1
1984	54.1
1986	55.7
1988	57.7
1990	59.5

SOURCE: AMERICAN PETROLEUM INSTITUTE, BASIC PETROLEUM DATA BOOK (1992)

World Net Electricity from Nuclear Power Plants, 1950–1990

Year	Capacity (megawatts)
1950	0
1952	0
1954	5
1956	50
1958	190
1960	830
1962	1800
1964	3100
1966	6200
1968	9200
1970	16 000
1972	32 000
1974	61 000
1976	85 000
1978	114 000
1980	135 000
1982	170 000
1984	219 000
1986	276 000
1988	311 000
1990	329 000
1991	326 000

SOURCE: U.S. DEPT. OF ENERGY, *International Energy Annual 1990* (1992) AND WORLDWATCH INSTITUTE, WORLD NUCLEAR INDUSTRY STATUS REPORT: 1992 (1992)

Energy Consumption Per Person, 1979–1989

Country	Gigajoules Used, 1989	Percent Change Since 1979
Australia	211	19
Brazil	23	3
Canada	321	4
Chile	35	22
China	23	40
Columbia	24	8
Cuba	45	9
Egypt	22	52
France	115	–14
Guatemala	6	–35
India	9	57
Italy	111	12
Japan	118	5
Libya	117	79
Mexico	51	13
Philippines	9	–14
Saudi Arabia	176	145
Somalia	2	103
Spain	73	5
Sri Lanka	3	1
Tunisia	21	16
United Arab Emirates	581	119
United Kingdom	147	–3
United States	295	–7
USSR	191	16

SOURCE: UNITED NATIONS STATISTICAL OFFICE

Case Study 3

A BURNING QUESTION

Forms and Dangers of Hazardous Waste

The EPA says that hazardous waste is:

any waste or combination of wastes that poses a substantial danger, now or in the future, to human, plant, or animal life and which therefore cannot be handled or disposed of without special precautions.

The EPA goes on to describe the forms and dangers of hazardous wastes:

Hazardous wastes are with us as solids, liquids, gases, and sludges. They may be toxic chemicals, acids, or caustics. They may catch fire or explode at normal temperatures and pressures or when exposed to air or water. Some may be set off by an electrostatic charge, others by being dropped or jarred. Some are highly sensitive to heat and friction. Hazardous wastes come in many other forms: biological materials, chemical and biological warfare agents, and radioactive materials.

It is difficult to identify hazardous compounds. That is because most problems associated with them result from long-term, low-level exposure. People who are exposed to dangerous chemicals usually are also exposed to a wide variety of other chemicals at the same time. In addition, if these chemicals act together, the effect may be greater than if they were acting individually. Most of the effects of hazardous chemicals don't show up until many years after exposure. In addition, the sensitivity to different substances varies among individuals.

Superfund

In 1980, Congress enacted the Comprehensive Environmental Response, Compensation, and Liability Act, better known as the Superfund. In 1986, the $10.1 billion fund was renewed. It is to be used for the cleanup of abandoned or inactive hazardous waste dump sites that are a threat to human health and the environment. The Environmental Protection Agency estimated that there are more than 32 000 sites in the United States containing potentially hazardous waste. As of February 1992, the EPA has placed 1183 sites on a priority cleanup list. These sites have a particularly high potential for harming nearby populations, groundwater, surface water, and the air. As of this writing, 50 sites on the EPA priority list have been declared clean, and 24 have been removed from the list.

Organic and Inorganic Compounds

Because there are so many carbon compounds, their study has become a branch of chemistry. Organic chemistry is the field of chemistry that is devoted to the study of carbon compounds. Organic materials always contain carbon, which is nearly always combined with hydrogen.

Hydrocarbons — such as coal, petroleum, and natural gas — are organic compounds. Caffeine, alcohol, and nylon are also organic. Another major division of chemistry, called inorganic chemistry, deals with the study of all other elements and their compounds. Minerals, rocks, and sand are inorganic.

States with Most National Priority List Hazardous Waste Sites, 1992

State	Nonfederal	Federal	Total
New Jersey	102	6	108
Pennsylvania	90	4	94
California	67	20	87
New York	79	4	83
Michigan	77	0	77
Florida	47	4	51
Washington	31	14	45
Minnesota	39	2	41
Wisconsin	39	0	39
Illinois	32	4	36

SOURCE: ENVIRONMENTAL PROTECTION AGENCY, 1992

Case Study 4

ACID ON THE WIND

The pH Scale

The pH scale is a way of describing a water solution in terms of how acidic or basic (alkaline) it is. An *acid* is a substance that produces hydrogen ions (H^+) in water solution. A *base* is a substance that produces hydroxide ions (OH^-) in solution. The pH scale is a way of indicating the concentrations of hydrogen ions and hydroxide ions in solutions. The scale has a range of 0 to 14. A solution having a pH at 7, the midpoint of the range, has equal concentrations of hydrogen ions (acid) and hydroxide ions (base). Such a solution is neither acid nor base. It is said to be neutral. Pure, distilled water has a pH of 7.

Adding acid (hydrogen ions) to pure water upsets the balance between hydrogen ions and hydroxide ions. As the concentration of hydrogen ions increases, the pH of the solution decreases. Normal rainfall is weakly acidic. It has a pH of 5.6. Battery acid with a pH of 0.3 has a relatively high concentration of hydrogen ions.

Values on the pH scale between 7 to 14 indicate that there are more hydroxide ions in solution than there are hydrogen ions. Solutions in this range of the scale are said to be basic or alkaline. A highly alkaline solution containing lime has a pH of 12.4, while one containing baking soda has a pH of 8.2

Pollution Credits

To help power companies deal with the financial burden of upgrading their facilities, an amendment to the 1990 Clean Air Act provides each power plant with an emission allowance. The emission allowance, determined individually for each company, gives the company permission to pollute up to a certain level. Each company is expected not to exceed its limit. A fine of $2000 is levied for every ton of emissions beyond the assigned limit. If a company can lower its emissions below its allowed limit, that company may sell the remaining unused allowance to another company. There is no set limit on the amount of emission credits that a company can purchase.

This innovative plan is built on the idea that a certain level of pollution is acceptable. In the past, the Federal Government set pollution standards for all utility companies and fined them if they did not comply. Now the new amendment gives companies another option. If they decide not to take action to reduce their emissions, they can buy pollution credits from companies that are running clean. The amendment assumes that companies will do whatever is most profitable. For the company selling the credits, there is the incentive of increased profits.

It is still an open question as to how a market in pollution credits will work. Some environmentalists in eastern areas are concerned that midwest industries may become the largest buyers of pollution credits. If the price of pollution credits is low, midwest companies may have less incentive to act to reduce acid rain. If that should become true, the Adirondacks may not benefit as much from the Clean Air Act as was once hoped.

Sulfur Emissions, 1970–89
(thousands of metric tons of SO_2)

	1970	1975	1980	1985	1989
Germany	3743	3334	3200	2400	1500
United Kingdom	6424	5370	4848	3676	3552
United States	28 400	25 900	23 400	21 100	20 700*

*1988 FIGURE

SOURCE: CO-OPERATIVE PROGRAMME FOR MONITORING AND EVALUATION OF THE LONG RANGE TRANSMISSION OF AIR POLLUTANTS IN EUROPE (EMEP); AND THE ORGANISATION FOR ECONOMIC CO-OPERATION AND DEVELOPMENT (OECD)

Nitrogen Emissions
(thousands of metric tons of NO_2)

	1970	1975	1980	1985	1989
Germany	2381	2571	2980	2950	3000
United Kingdom	2510	2427	2442	2278	2513
United States	18 300	19 200	20 400	19 800	19 800*

*1988 FIGURE

SOURCE: CO-OPERATIVE PROGRAMME FOR MONITORING AND EVALUATION OF THE LONG RANGE TRANSMISSION OF AIR POLLUTANTS IN EUROPE (EMEP); AND THE ORGANISATION FOR ECONOMIC CO-OPERATION AND DEVELOPMENT (OECD)

Estimated and Projected Population Size by Region, 1950–2025

	Population (millions)				
Region	1950	1970	1990	2000	2025
Industrialized countries	832	1049	1207	1264	1354
Developing countries	1684	2649	4086	4997	7150
World Total	2516	3698	5292	6261	8504

Source: United Nations Population Division, World Population Prospects 1990 (United Nations, New York 1991)

Share of World Population by Region, 1950–2025

	% Share of World Population				
Region	1950	1970	1990	2000	2025
Industrialized countries	33.1	28.4	22.8	20.2	15.9
Developing countries	66.9	71.6	77.2	79.8	84.1
World Total	100.0	100.0	100.0	100.0	100.0

Source: United Nations Population Division, World Population Prospects 1990 (United Nations, New York 1991)

Emissions Estimates for EPA-Monitored Pollutants by Source, 1985–1990 (million metric tons)

Year	Transportation	Fuel Combustion	Industrial Processes	Solid Waste	Miscellaneous	Total*
Sulfur Oxides						
1985	0.9	17.0	3.2	0.0	0.0	20.9
1990	0.9	17.1	3.1	0.0	0.0	21.2
Carbon Monoxide						
1985	47.9	7.5	4.4	1.9	7.1	68.7
1990	37.6	7.5	4.7	1.7	8.6	60.1
Nitrogen Oxides						
1985	8.9	10.2	0.6	0.1	0.2	19.9
1990	7.5	11.2	0.6	0.1	0.3	19.6
Ozone						
1985	7.6	0.9	8.5	0.6	2.5	20.1
1990	6.4	0.9	8.1	0.6	2.7	18.7
Particulates						
1985	1.3	1.1	2.7	0.3	0.7	6.0
1990	1.5	1.1	2.7	0.2	0.9	6.4

* The sums of subcategories may not equal the Total due to rounding of numbers.

Source: Environmental Protection Agency, National Air Quality and Emissions Trends Report, 1990 (1992)

Case Study 5

SOMETHING IN THE WATER

Groundwater

The water that falls to Earth soaks into the ground and is pulled downward by gravity until it reaches an impermeable layer. This impermeable layer may be a bed of shale, or unweathered, nonporous bedrock. The water, unable to continue soaking downward, starts to fill the pores in the rock or soil. The area of the rock or soil where the pores are completely filled by groundwater is called the *zone of saturation*. The top of this zone is called the *water table*. As more water soaks into the ground, the zone of saturation gets thicker and the water table rises, getting closer to Earth's surface.

Not all the groundwater is stored in the zone of saturation. Some water is left behind in the soil and rock as the water moves downward. This water is trapped where grains are in contact and is therefore not pulled downward by gravity. This water is only removed by evaporation or by plant roots. The layer of rock or soil above the water table is called the *zone of aeration*. *Aerate* means to add air to something.

Aquifers are underground deposits of sand, gravel, or rock through which water passes easily. Aquifers are the water-bearing rocks that are drilled into for water wells. When water is removed from the aquifer, the water table drops. Rainfall can refill, or recharge, an aquifer If groundwater is withdrawn from an aquifer or the zone of saturation faster than it is being replaced by precipitation, several things can happen. Along coastal regions, salt water may begin to replace the fresh groundwater, making wells unusable. If enough groundwater is pumped out with no water coming in to replace it, the wells will go dry. Soil and rock may settle or collapse, causing a sinkhole.

Groundwater pollutants are removed by filtering and by the destructive action of bacteria. The faster water moves through an aquifer, the more quickly pollutants are filtered out or are broken down. Groundwater may move as quickly as one meter per day just below Earth's surface or as slowly as one meter per year within deeply buried rocks. Groundwater can move too slowly to effectively rid itself of even minor concentrations of pollutants.

Estimated Water Use in the United States, 1965–1985				
1965	1970	1975	1980	1985
Population (in millions)				
194	206	216	230	242
Groundwater used (in billions of liters per day)				
226	257	309	313	275
Surface water used (in billions of liters per day)				
792	943	981	1094	943
SOURCE: UNITED STATES GEOLOGICAL SURVEY, CIRCULAR 1004, ESTIMATED USE OF WATER (1987)				

GROUNDWATER

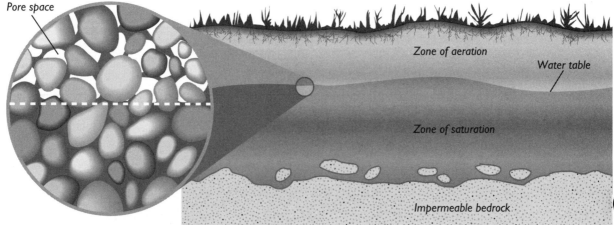

Case Study 6
NO ROOM IN THE BIN

Sanitary Landfills

In the past, solid waste was disposed of in open landfills commonly called dumps. In addition to being ugly and smelly, these landfills were a source of groundwater pollution. Water that fell on these landfills as rain or snow sank through the garbage, mixing with the moisture that got pushed out of the garbage as it was compressed. This liquid — called leachate — carried toxic chemicals into the groundwater. It also carried with it more than 100 different types of viruses from sources such as disposable diapers.

Modern landfills are commonly called sanitary landfills. Sites for sanitary landfills are carefully chosen to minimize environmental damage. The landfill has a lower impermeable liner or liners. Leachate cannot get through the liner and into the groundwater. Instead the leachate is collected, pumped out of the landfill, and treated. Groundwater around the landfill site is carefully monitored to detect leaks. In a humid environment, the ideal sanitary landfill is built over impermeable bedrock, such as shale or clay. This naturally prevents leaking leachate from entering the groundwater. Workers cover the solid waste with soil every day to reduce both odor and pest populations.

The decomposition of buried solid waste releases explosive methane gas and poisonous hydrogen sulfide gas. These gases can seep out of a landfill. Both gases are heavier than air and will accumulate in low spots, including nearby basements. Other gases, such as ammonia and nitrogen compounds, are also produced. A well-designed sanitary landfill also collects and removes these gases.

U.S. Municipal Solid Waste
(% of total generation)

Category	Year			
	1960	1970	1980	1988
Materials Recovered	6.7	7.1	9.7	13.1
for recycling	6.7	7.1	9.7	12.9
for composting	0.0	0.0	0.0	0.2
Incinerated	30.8	20.6	9.2	14.2
with energy recovery	0.0	0.3	1.8	13.6
without energy recovery	30.8	20.3	7.4	0.6
Landfill or Other	62.5	72.4	81.1	72.7
Total Generation	100.0	100.0	100.0	100.0

SOURCE: U.S. ENVIRONMENTAL PROTECTION AGENCY, CHARACTERIZATION OF MUNICIPAL SOLID WASTE IN THE UNITED STATES: 1990 UPDATE (1990)

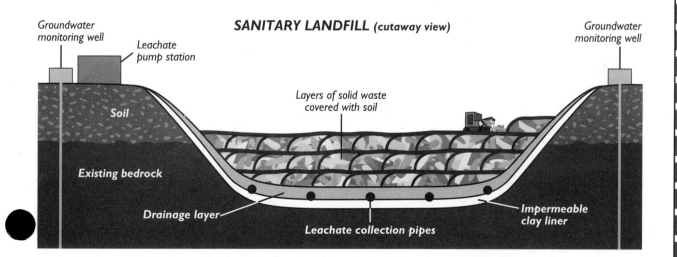

SANITARY LANDFILL (cutaway view)

Case Study 7

RAIN FORESTS UNDER SIEGE

Living Communities

Life on Earth exists in a thin layer of soil, water, and air known as the *biosphere*. The biosphere extends from about 11 kilometers deep in the oceans to about 8 kilometers high in the atmosphere. The biosphere has all the materials and conditions needed to support life.

The biosphere is divided into units called biomes. A *biome* is a geographical region with a characteristic group of plants and animals. Usually a biome on land is named for the dominant vegetation it contains. A grassland biome, for example, contains mainly grasses. Aquatic biomes are identified by their dominant animal populations. Land or terrestrial biomes you may recognize are tundra, taiga, temperate deciduous forest, tropical rain forest, and desert.

Scientists divide biomes into ecosystems. An *ecosystem* is a unit of the biosphere where organisms interact with one another and with the environment. Usually an ecosystem has some sort of natural boundary. For example, a single tide pool that forms on a beach at low tide is an ecosystem. Ecosystems may be large, like a forest, or small, like a rotting log.

Different organisms live within an ecosystem. Organisms living in one part of the ecosystem are not normally found in other parts. The part of the ecosystem in which an organism lives is its *habitat*. The role each organism carries out in its habitat is called its *niche*. You can think of a niche as an organism's occupation and its habitat as its address.

Extinction

Extinction, or the dying off of a species from Earth, is a continuously occurring process. Species have been evolving and becoming extinct since life began on Earth over 600 million years ago. Some extinctions occur when changes in the local environment put so much stress on a species that it can no longer live. Extinctions of many species at one time, called *mass extinctions,* have occurred at many times in Earth's past. A well-known mass extinction occurred 65 million years ago. It was this event that caused the extinction of the dinosaurs and other groups of animals and plants at the end of the Cretaceous Period. This mass extinction is thought to have been caused by the impact on Earth of a large asteroid.

Human activities have led to extinctions and are pushing many other species close to extinction. The largest cause of extinction is habitat destruction. Habitat destruction occurs when people clear land for agriculture, construction, or for other purposes.

Tropical Deforestation

Region	Area with forest 1980 (hectares)	Area with forest 1990 (hectares)	Area deforested annually 1980's
Central America & Mexico	77 000	63 500	1400
Caribbean	48 800	47 100	200
Tropical South America	797 100	729 300	6800
South Asia	70 600	66 200	400
Continental Southeast Asia	83 200	69 700	1300
Southeast Asia islands	157 000	138 900	1800
Northwest Africa	41 900	38 000	400
Northeast Africa	92 300	85 300	700
West Africa	55 200	43 400	1200
Central Africa	230 100	215 400	1500
Tropical Southern Africa	217 700	206 300	1100
Madagascar	13 200	11 700	200

SOURCE: WORLD RESOURCES INSTITUTE, WORLD RESOURCES 1992–93 (1992)

Case Study 8

TROUBLE IN THE SOUND

Estuaries

Estuaries form where fresh water and salt water mix— for example, at the mouth of a river or in a salt marsh. Estuaries are more productive biomes than either the ocean or fresh water, but life is not as diverse as in fresh water or the open ocean. The water in an estuary is shallow, allowing light to penetrate to the bottom. Plant life is varied and abundant. Marsh grasses and other forms of rooted vegetation ring the shore. Algae coat the rocks, and plankton thrive in the open water. Tidal currents constantly mix the water, keeping nutrients dispersed in the estuary's waters.

Estuaries support many types of animals. Oysters, clams, and mussels are the most common animals. Snails live among the marsh grasses. Bottom-dwellers include sponges and worms. Many types of fish either live in the estuary or use it as a nursery. Many water birds use estuaries as feeding grounds either year-round or during seasonal migration.

The Water Cycle

Each day a trillion (1 000 000 000 000) metric tons of Earth's water changes to water vapor. Most of that water vapor evaporates from the ocean, lakes, rivers, and from the soil. A smaller amount of water vapor is given off by plants and animals. For example, the leaves of one large oak tree release up to 150 000 liters of water into the air each year.

The air containing the water vapor cools as it rises through the atmosphere. As the air cools, the water vapor condenses to form cloud droplets. If enough cloud droplets join together, the water falls back to Earth as some form of precipitation. Most of this precipitation — about 70 percent — evaporates from the ground where it falls. Some of the rain sinks into the ground, where it becomes groundwater. Some of the rain runs off along or just beneath the ground's surface into rivers and lakes and returns to the ocean, where it is eventually turned back into water vapor. The process by which water evaporates from Earth's surface, condenses into clouds, falls as precipitation, and then evaporates again is called the water cycle.

For Earth as a whole, the amount of water that returns to the ground as precipitation is the same as the amount that evaporates. The small amount of water broken down into hydrogen and oxygen each year is replaced by new water from volcanic eruptions. In effect, there is no new water being added to the water cycle.

Water Quality in Selected States

State	Miles of Rivers Tested	Miles of Rivers Fishable
Alaska	N/A	N/A
Arkansas	11 310	9426
California	11 448	9069
Connecticut	893	664
Florida	7950	6750
Georgia	20 000	19 395
Illinois	13 123	11 476
Iowa	7155	90
Louisiana	8535	6510
Massachusetts	1623	1061
Minnesota	6079	2292
Missouri	21 063	11 216
Nevada	1559	793
New Mexico	3117	2851
New York	70 000	69 300
Ohio	7688	2524
South Carolina	3594	3230
Tennessee	11 081	10 857
Texas	16 203	16 044
Vermont	5266	4468
Washington	5141	2873

SOURCE: U.S. ENVIRONMENTAL PROTECTION AGENCY, NATIONAL WATER QUALITY INVENTORY: 1990 REPORT TO CONGRESS (MARCH, 1992)

Appendix

Expressing an Educated Opinion

Writing a position letter

Public officials — such as your Senators and Representative — pay attention to the mail and phone calls they receive. Even if you can't vote yet, you are being represented by these officials. You have a right to express your opinion to them on environmental issues with which you are concerned.

The key to effective lobbying is to express yourself clearly and briefly. Here are a few other tips for writing an effective position letter:

- Remember that you can write to support an official's position just as easily as you can write to disagree. You may also write to ask what that official's position is on an issue.

- Try to keep your letter to one typewritten page. If you are writing the letter longhand, write legibly.

- An effective letter would tell the official how the issue affects you and others. Be realistic and cite your evidence.

These suggestions would also apply to a Letter to the Editor for a newspaper, journal, or magazine.

Writing for information

Many environmental organizations are lobbying groups that have information available to the public. Other groups only provide information to members, in the form of newsletters, mailings, or pamphlets. Do not be disappointed if you request information from a group and only receive information about how to become a member. Many of these groups operate on small budgets and cannot afford to send out large amounts of literature.

Remember that you are more likely to get the information you want if you ask for a *specific* piece of information. For instance, if you are interested in acid rain, you need to clearly request information on acid rain, not on Earth's environment in general.

How to write a business letter

The letter you will write to express an opinion or to request information is a business letter. Business letters follow this format:

Your street address
Your town, state, and zip code
Date

Name of the person to whom you are writing
Name of the organization
Street address
Town, state, and zip code

Dear Mr./Ms./Dr./Congressman _____:

Introductory paragraph
  Quickly say why you are writing. This gives the person reading the letter an idea for what type of information you are asking or the issue on which you want to voice an opinion. If you are writing about a specific bill or piece of legislation, mention it by name or number. If you are asking for information, you will not need more than this paragraph and a conclusion.

Body of the letter
  State your position on the issue. Support your position with facts and personal experience.

Conclusion
  Summarize what you have said. Thank the person for their time.

Sincerely,
  Leave four blank lines here so that you will have room to sign your name.

Type or print your name here

ADDRESSES

If you are writing to elected officials in the United States federal government, you may find the following addresses useful:

The President or Vice-President:
President (full name of President) or Vice-President (full name of Vice-President)
The White House
Washington, DC 20500

Senators:
The Honorable (full name of Senator)
United States Senate
Washington, DC 20510

Representatives:
The Honorable (full name of Representative)
House of Representatives
Washington, DC 20515

Resources for Further Study

The following organizations and government agencies are just a small selection of many groups that can provide you with information on environmental issues. When researching an environmental issue, be sure to contact a variety of sources. Try to get the facts from different sides of an issue in order to make an informed decision.

For more information about these groups or about the issues with which they are concerned, write to them at the following addresses. Apply the same analytical and critical thinking skills to the materials you receive from them as you applied to the case studies presented in this book.

Citizen's Clearinghouse for
  Hazardous Waste
Center for Environmental Justice
P.O. Box 6806
Falls Church, VA 22040

Conservation International
1015 18th Street NW
Suite 1000
Washington, DC 20036

Cultural Survival, Inc.
215 First Street
Cambridge, MA 02142
(Information on indigenous people and the rain forest)

Cultural Survival, Inc., Canada
1 Nicholas Street
Suite 420
Ottawa, Canada K1N7B7
(Information on James Bay)

EARTHWATCH
P.O. Box 403 Dept. HS
Watertown, MA 02272
(Sponsors short-term scientific expeditions with noted scholars worldwide in subjects from archaeology to zoology)

The Environmental Exchange
1718 Connecticut Ave. NW
Suite 600
Washington, DC 20009

Environmental Protection Agency
Office of Environmental Education
  Division
(A-107)
401 M Street SW
Washington, DC 20460

Greenpeace, Inc.
1436 U Street NW
Washington, DC 20009
(Concerned with toxic waste, nuclear issues, ocean and atmospheric ecology)

Institute for Environmental
  Education
18554 Haskins Rd.
Chagrin Falls, OH 44023

National Audubon Society
Attn: Conservation Information
700 Broadway
New York, NY 10003

National Energy Information Center
EI-231
Forrestal Bldg, Room IF-048
1000 Independence Ave. SW
Washington, DC 20585

Nuclear Information and Resource
  Service
1424 16th Street NW
Suite 601
Washington, DC 20036

Rainforest Action Network
450 Sansome
Suite 700
San Francisco, CA 94111

Renew America
1400 16th Street NW
Suite 710
Washington, DC 20036
(Summary of current environmental conditions)

Rodale Institute
222 Main Street
Emmaus, PA 18098

Soil and Water Conservation Society
7515 NE Ankeny Rd.
Ankeny, IA 50021

Stream Watch
Izaak Walton League of America
1401 Wilson Blvd.
Level B
Arlington, VA 22209
(Include a self-addressed, stamped envelope to receive "Save the Streams" booklet and student packet)

U.S. Bureau of Mines
Office of Public Information
810 7th Street NW
Washington, DC 20241

U.S. Fish and Wildlife Service
Publications Office
4040 N. Fairfax Dr.
130 Webb Bldg.
Arlington, VA 22203
(Endangered species and habitat conservation)

Vermont Institute of Natural
  Science
P.O. Box 86
Woodstock, VT 05091
(Solid waste management)

World Wildlife Fund
1250 24th Street NW
Suite 400
Washington, DC 20037
(Rain forest and biodiversity issues. Will provide information on their organizaton.)

Graphing Skills

You use a line graph when you are comparing two continuously changing values. For example, the table below shows data for two changing quantities: the year and the amount of an ozone-destroying chlorofluorocarbon (CFC-12) released into Earth's atmosphere in that year. Both values are changing, so a line graph is appropriate for graphing these data.

CFC-12 Emission Data	
Year	CFC-12 Released (millions of kg)
1982	337.4
1984	359.4
1986	376.5
1988	392.8

When making a line graph from a table of data, follow these general rules.

1. *Put a title on your graph.* The title tells your reader what the graph is about. Print the title at the top of your graph paper.

2. *Leave space for axis labels.* Leave some space between the edge of your paper and the horizontal and vertical axes.

3. *Decide which quantity to plot on the horizontal axis and which quantity to plot on the vertical axis.* Sometimes, one of the two quantities is being changed by you in a regular way. This would be called the controlled quantity and you would plot it along the horizontal axis. Label the vertical axis with the other quantity. In this sample, the year should go along the horizontal axis.

4. *Choose a scale for each axis.* The scales on the two axes do not have to be the same. Your scale should do two things. First, it must allow you to plot all the

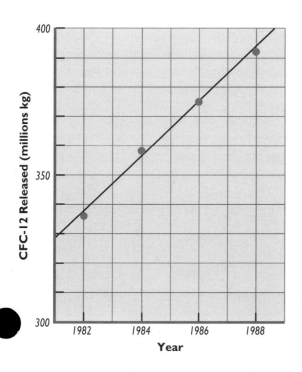

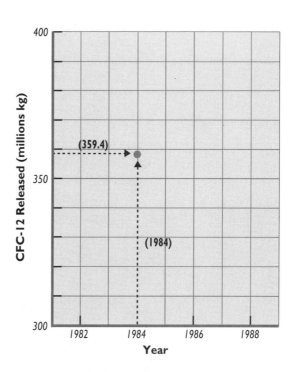

data. Therefore, the scale must have a range wide enough to include the highest and lowest data. Second, the scale should be easy to use. Make each square of your graph paper stand for a multiple of 1, 2, 5, 10, and so on. Once you have chosen your scales, clearly mark them along the axes of your graph.

5. *Plot your data.* On a line graph, each data point is a combination of two values—one for each axis. To plot a data point, first find its horizontal axis value on the scale. Look at the second piece of data in the table. The year value is 1984. Follow that value up from the horizontal axis until you are across from the vertical axis value for that data point. In this case, the vertical axis value for 1984 is 359.4 million kg. Where the horizontal and vertical axes meet, make a small dot or x. Plot all of the available data points in the same manner.

6. *Look at the data points to determine the pattern.* Often data points will appear to fall along a straight line. Other times the points will follow a smooth curve.

7. *Draw a line or curve to show the general trend of the data points.* Science data points are usually measured data. All measurements have some error. Therefore, measured data seldom fall exactly on a straight line, even if the points at first appear to fall on a straight line. Rather than connecting each data point, draw a straight line or a curve that best fits the data points. A good best-fit line often passes through some points, but also has some points above it and some below it.

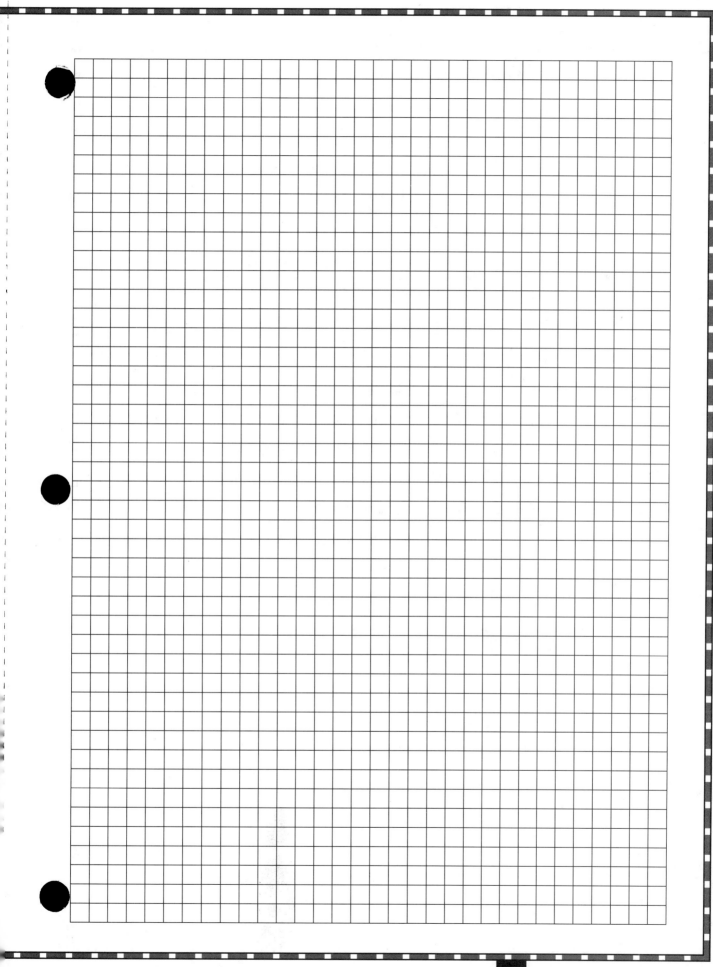

Photo Credits

Picture Research: Sue McDermott

Cover Photographs: Terry Donnelly (Tom Stack & Associates); *earth* © Telegraph Colour Library 199, FPG International

2: *t* Runk/Schoenberger (Grant Heilman Photography); *b* NASA. **3:** Grant Heilman (Grant Heilman Photography). **4:** Stephen J. Krasemann (DRK Photo). **5-6:** Grant Heilman (Grant Heilman Photography). **7:** Peter Beck (The Stock Market). **9:** *l* Bob Daemmrich (Stock Boston); *r* NASA. **11:** Richard B. Levine. **13:** M.I. Walker (Photo Researchers, Inc.). **14:** J. Berndt (Stock Boston). **17:** *l* Peter Menzel (Stock Boston); *r* Lionel J.M. Delevingne (Stock Boston). **19:** Rick McIntyre. **20:** Stephen Homer (First Light). **22:** Lionel J.M. Delevingne (Stock Boston). **24:** Lisa Law (The Image Works). **27:** *l* Gary Milburn (Tom Stack & Associates); *r* Robert Visser (Greenpeace). **28:** *t* Richard B. Levine; *b* John Shaw (Tom Stack & Associates. **29:** Barbara Alper (Stock Boston). **35:** *l* Michael Gadomsk (Earth Scenes); *r* Joe Sohm (The Image Works). **38:** Fredrik D. Bodin (Stock Boston). **39:** Dr. D.W. Schindler (First Light). **40:** Richard Pasley (Stock Boston). **43:** *l* Grant Heilman (Grant Heilman Photography); *r* Michael A. Keller (The Stock Market). **46:** *t* Inga Spence (Tom Stack & Associates); *b* John H. Gerard from National Audobon Society (Photo Researchers, Inc.). **47:** Larry Lefever (Grant Heilman Photography). **48:** Chris Collins (The Stock Market). **51:** *l* Richard B. Levine; *r* Dennis Capolongo (Black Star). **52:** W. Hill, Jr. (The Image Works). **53:** Rob Crandall (Stock Boston). **57:** Thomas Kitchen (Tom Stack & Associates). **61:** *l* D. Cavagnaro (DRK Photo); *r* Michael Dwyer (Stock Boston). **64:** Tom McHugh (Photo Researchers, Inc.). **66:** Leonide Principe (Photo Researchers, Inc.). **69:** *l* Rafael Macia (Photo Researchers, Inc.); *r* Charles Gatewood (Stock Boston). **70:** Tom Stack (Tom Stack & Associates). **72:** Daniel S. Brody (Stock Boston). **73:** Pedrick (The Image Works). **74:** Lawrence Migdale.